**Jungian Psychology
Unplugged**

Marie-Louise von Franz, Honorary Patron

**Studies in Jungian Psychology
by Jungian Analysts**

Daryl Sharp, General Editor

Jungian Psychology Unplugged

My Life As an Elephant

Daryl Sharp

To friends, relatives, elephants and fish, and especially to
Marie-Louise von Franz (1915-1998), to whom I owe so much.

See the Bibliography for other titles by this author.

Canadian Cataloguing in Publication Data

Sharp, Daryl, 1936-
  Jungian psychology unplugged: my life as an elephant

(Studies in Jungian psychology by Jungian analysts; 80)

Includes bibliographical references and index.

ISBN 0-919123-81-3

1. Jung, C.G. (Carl Gustav), 1875-1961.
2. Psychoanalysis. I. Title. II. Series.

BF173.S525 1998   150.19'54   C98-930317-9

INNER CITY BOOKS
Box 1271, Station Q, Toronto, ON M4T 2P4, Canada
Telephone (416) 927-0355 / Fax (416) 924-1814
Web site: www.inforamp.net/~icb / E-mail: icb@inforamp.net

Honorary Patron: Marie-Louise von Franz.
Publisher and General Editor: Daryl Sharp.
Senior Editor: Vicki Cowan.

INNER CITY BOOKS was founded in 1980 to promote the
understanding and practical application of the work of C.G. Jung.

Cover illustrations:
Top: "Running Scared." Watercolor by Canadian artist Joyce
    Young, © 1993. (Author's collection)
Bottom: "We Are Keepers of Ancient Secrets / For we walked
    the world when it was new." (Eileen Lynch) Photograph
    by Jack Rosen, © 1979 Freelance Inc.
Back Cover: "My pal the elephant." © Mike Hollist 1982/Daily Mail, UK.

Index by the author.

Printed and bound in Canada by University of Toronto Press

CONTENTS

Preface

On a dreary afternoon in the fall of 1974 I was walking in the hills of Zurich, feeling bleak and very sorry for myself, when I spied an object on the path. I stooped down and picked it up. It was a little black elephant made of ebony. It was numinous to me, a magical thing. On the spot, I fell in love.

I took it to be a case of what Jung calls synchronicity, where an outer event coincides with what is going on inside. I assumed it had something to do with my psychology and I spent the next few years exploring what that might be.

I went to see elephants in the zoo; I read books about them; I collected them. Friends and relatives overwhelmed me with elephants of all sizes and materials and numerous objects incorporating their shape. I painted pictures of elephants and my dreams were full of them.

Now I have a pretty good idea of what elephants have to do with me and why I found that first one. I was thirty-eight years old at the time. I had burned my bridges and I was on my knees. I had gone to Switzerland to begin training at the C.G. Jung Institute of Zurich. A lot has happened to me since, but much of it has to do, metaphorically, with elephants.

*

This book brings together and updates the essence of my writings on Jungian psychology over the past twenty years, from typology, complexes and relationship, to individuation and the dynamics of neurosis. As always, my intention has been simply to present a comprehensive overview of Jung's basic concepts and their application.

C.G. Jung at the age of 75

1
Psychological Types

*Classification does not explain the
individual psyche. Nevertheless, an understanding of
psychological types opens the way to a better
understanding of human psychology in general.*
—C.G. Jung.

The experience that not everyone functions in the same way has been the basis for numerous systems of typology. From earliest times, attempts have been made to categorize individual attitudes and behavior patterns in order to explain the differences between people.

The oldest known system of typology is the one devised by oriental astrologers. They classified character in terms of four trigons, corresponding to the four elements—water, air, earth and fire. The air trigon in the horoscope, for instance, consists of the three aerial signs of the zodiac, Aquarius, Gemini, Libra; the fire trigon is made up of Aries, Leo and Sagittarius. According to this age-old view, whoever is born under these signs shares in their aerial or fiery nature and has a corresponding temperament and fate; similarly for the water and earth signs. This system survives in modified form in present-day astrology.

Closely connected with this ancient cosmological scheme is the physiological typology of Greek medicine, according to which individuals were classified as phlegmatic, sanguine, choleric or melancholic, based on the designations for the secretions of the body (phlegm, blood, yellow bile and black bile). These descriptions are still in common linguistic use, though medically they have long since been superseded.

Jung's own model of typology grew out of an extensive historical review of the type question in literature, mythology, aesthetics, philosophy and psychopathology. In the preface to *Psychological Types,* which contains his scholarly research and a detailed summary of his conclusions, he writes:

This book is the fruit of nearly twenty years' work in the domain of practical psychology. It grew gradually in my thoughts, taking shape from the countless impressions and experiences of a psychiatrist in the treatment of nervous illnesses, from intercourse with men and women of all social levels, from my personal dealings with friend and foe alike, and, finally, from a critique of my own psychological peculiarities.[1]

Jung's model of types is not a system of character analysis, nor is it a way of labeling oneself or others. Much as one might use a compass to determine where one is in the physical world, Jung's typology is a tool for psychological orientation, a guide to understanding both oneself and many of the difficulties that arise in relationships.

Jung's Basic Model

Whereas the earlier classifications were based on observations of temperamental or emotional behavior patterns, Jung's model is concerned with the movement of psychic energy and the way in which one habitually, or by preference, orients oneself in the world.

From this point of view, Jung differentiates eight typological groups: two personality attitudes—*introversion* and *extraversion*—and four functions (modes of orientation)—*thinking, sensation, intuition* and *feeling*—each of which may operate in an introverted or extraverted way.

Thanks to Jung's writings, introversion and extraversion have become household words, but their meaning is frequently misunderstood; the four functions are not so widely known and are even less understood.

Introversion and extraversion are psychological modes of adaptation. In the former, the movement of energy is toward the inner world. In the latter, interest is directed toward the outer world. In one case the subject (one's own inner reality) and in the other the object (things and other people, outer reality) is of primary importance.

Introversion, according to Jung, is characterized by a reflective, retiring nature that dislikes or distrusts change and is always slightly on the defensive. Conversely, *extraversion* is characterized by an outgoing, candid and accommodating nature that adapts easily to a given situation,

---

[1] *Psychological Types,* CW 6, p. xi. [CW refers throughout to *The Collected Works of C.G. Jung*]

quickly forms attachments and with little forethought ventures forth into unknown situations.

In the extraverted attitude, external factors are the predominant starting point for judgments, perceptions, feelings and actions. This sharply contrasts with the nature of introversion, where subjective factors are the chief motivation.

Extraverts like to travel, to meet new people, see new places. They are the typical adventurers, the life of the party, open and friendly. The introvert is essentially conservative, preferring the familiar surroundings of home, intimate times with a few close friends. To the extravert, the introvert is a stick-in-the-mud, a spoil-sport, dull and predictable. The introvert, who has a more limited horizon and generally feels self-sufficient, might describe the latter as flighty, a superficial gadabout.

In practice, it is not possible to demonstrate the introverted and extraverted attitudes per se, that is in isolation. Whether a person is one way or the other only becomes apparent in association with one of the four functions (modes of orientation), each of which has its special area of expertise.

The function of *thinking* refers to the process of cognitive thought; *sensation* is perception by means of the physical sense organs; *feeling* is the function of subjective judgment or valuation; and *intuition* refers to perception by way of the unconscious (e.g., receptivity to unconscious contents in oneself and in others).

Briefly, the sensation function establishes that something exists, thinking tells us what it is, feeling tells us what it's worth, and through intuition we have a sense of what can be done with it. Any one function by itself, writes Jung, is not sufficient for ordering our experience of ourselves or the world around us:

> For complete orientation all four functions should contribute equally: thinking should facilitate cognition and judgment, feeling should tell us how and to what extent a thing is important or unimportant for us, sensation should convey concrete reality to us through seeing, hearing, tasting, etc., and intuition should enable us to divine the hidden possibilities.[2]

---

[2] *Ibid.*, par. 900.

The Four Functions

Jung's basic model, including the relationship between the four functions, comprises a quaternity, as shown in the diagram below. Thinking is here arbitrarily placed at the top; any of the other functions might be placed there, according to which one a person most favors. The relative position of the other functions, however—which one is at the bottom and which two on the horizontal axis—are determined by the one at the top. (The reason for this, involving the nature of the individual functions, will soon become apparent.)

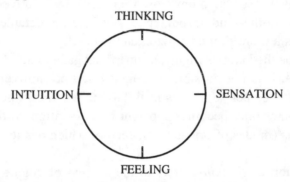

The ideal is to have conscious access to the function or functions appropriate in a given circumstance, but in practice the four functions are not equally at one's conscious disposal; that is, they are not uniformly developed or differentiated. Invariably one or the other is more developed, called the primary or superior function, while the rest remain inferior, relatively undifferentiated.

The terms "superior" and "inferior" in this context do not imply value judgments. No function is any better than any of the others. The superior function is simply the one a person is most likely to use; similarly, inferior does not mean pathological but merely unused or at least less used compared to the favored function.

What happens to those functions that are not consciously brought into daily use and therefore not developed?

They remain in a more or less primitive and infantile state, often only half conscious, or even quite unconscious. The relatively undeveloped functions constitute a specific inferiority which is characteristic of each type and is an integral part of his total character. The one-sided emphasis on thinking is always accompanied by an inferiority of feeling, and differentiated sensation is injurious to intuition and vice versa.[3]

Typologically, most people are a bowl of soup. They function in an introverted or extraverted way depending on their mood, the weather or their state of mind; they think, feel, sense and intuit more or less at random, being no better or worse at one function than any other, and having little inkling of the consequences. They may at first glance seem to be well rounded. However, such characteristics are typical of unconsciousness, for consciousness implies a certain differentiation in the way one functions. "The uniformly conscious or uniformly unconscious state of the functions," notes Jung, "is the mark of a primitive mentality."[4]

Rational and Irrational Functions

Jung further described two of the four functions as *rational* (or judging) and two as *irrational* (or perceiving).

Thinking, as a function of logical discrimination, is rational (judging). So is feeling, which as a way of evaluating our likes and dislikes can be quite as discriminating as thinking. Thinking and feeling are called rational because both are based on a reflective, linear process that coalesces into a particular judgment.

Sensation and intuition are the two functions Jung labeled as irrational (perceiving). Each is a way of perceiving simply what is—sensation sees what is in the external world, while intuition sees (or somehow "picks up") what is in the inner world.

The term "irrational," as applied to the functions of sensation and intuition, does not mean illogical or "crazy," but rather beyond or outside of reason. The physical perception of something does not depend on logic—things just *are*. Similarly, an intuition exists in itself; it is present in the mind, independent of reason or a rational process of thought. Jung comments:

---

[3] Ibid., par. 955.
[4] Ibid., par. 667.

Merely because [the irrational types] subordinate judgment to perception, it would be quite wrong to regard them as "unreasonable." It would be truer to say that they are in the highest degree *empirical.* They base themselves exclusively on experience—so exclusively that, as a rule, their judgment cannot keep pace with their experience.[5]

It is particularly important to distinguish between feeling as a psychological function and the many other common uses of the word. Jung acknowledged the possible confusion: we say we "feel" happy, sad, angry, regretful and so on; we have a "feeling" the weather will change or the stock market will fall; silk "feels" smoother than cotton, something does not "feel" right, etc. Clearly we use the word "feeling" quite loosely, since in a particular context it may refer to sense perception, thoughts, intuition or an emotional reaction.

Here it is a matter of clearly defining our terminology. We can measure temperature in degrees Fahrenheit, Celsius or Réaumur, distance in miles or kilometers, weight in ounces or grams, bulk in cups, bushels or pounds—so long as we indicate which system we are using. In Jung's model of typology, the term "feeling" refers strictly to the way in which we subjectively evaluate what something, or someone, is worth to us. This is the sense in which it is rational; in fact, to the extent that it is not colored by emotion, which is to say influenced by an activated complex, feeling can be quite cold.

Indeed, the feeling function, as a mode of psychological orientation, must above all not be confused with emotion. The latter, more properly called affect, is invariably the consequence of an active complex. "Feeling is distinguished from affect," writes Jung, "by the fact that it produces no perceptible physical innervations, i.e., neither more nor less than an ordinary thinking process."[6]

Affect tends to contaminate or distort each of the functions: we can't think straight when we are angry; happiness colors the way we perceive the world; we can't properly evaluate what something is worth to us when we're upset; and possibilities dry up when we're depressed.

---

[5] Ibid., par. 371.
[6] Ibid., par. 725.

The Primary Function and Auxiliary Functions

As noted above, one of the four functions is invariably more developed than the others. This is called the primary or superior function, the one we automatically use because it comes most naturally and brings certain rewards. Writes Jung:

> Experience shows that it is practically impossible, owing to adverse circumstances in general, for anyone to develop all his psychological functions simultaneously. The demands of society compel a man to apply himself first and foremost to the differentiation of the function with which he is best equipped by nature, or which will secure him the greatest social success. Very frequently, indeed as a general rule, a man identifies more or less completely with the most favoured and hence the most developed function. It is this that gives rise to the various psychological types. As a consequence of this one-sided development, one or more functions are necessarily retarded.[7]

The word "retarded" here means neglected or not developed. In fact only in extreme cases are the other functions completely absent. There is usually a second function (occasionally even a third) that is prominent enough to exert a co-determining influence on consciousness.

One can of course be conscious of the contents or products associated with each of the functions. For instance, I can know what I'm thinking without having a primary thinking function, and I can tell the difference between a table and a bottle without having a superior sensation function. But we can only speak of the "consciousness" of a function, according to Jung, "when its use is under the control of the will and, at the same time, its governing principle is the decisive one for the orientation of consciousness." He continues:

> This absolute sovereignty always belongs, empirically, to one function alone, and *can* belong only to one function, because the equally independent intervention of another function would necessarily produce a different orientation which, partially at least, would contradict the first. But since it is a vital condition for the conscious process of adaptation always to have clear and unambiguous aims, the presence of a second function of

---

[7] Ibid., par. 763.

equal power is naturally ruled out. This other function, therefore, can have only a secondary importance. . . . Its secondary importance is due to the fact that it is not, like the primary function . . . an absolutely reliable and decisive factor, but comes into play more as an auxiliary or complementary function.[8]

In practice, the auxiliary function is always one whose nature, rational or irrational, is different from the primary function. For instance, feeling cannot be the secondary function when thinking is dominant, and vice versa, because both are rational or judging functions:

Thinking, if it is to be real thinking and true to its own principle, must rigorously exclude feeling. This, of course, does not do away with the fact that there are individuals whose thinking and feeling are on the same level, both being of equal motive power for consciousness. But in these cases there is also no question of a differentiated type, but merely of relatively undeveloped thinking and feeling.[9]

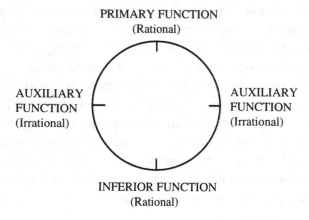

PRIMARY FUNCTION
(Rational)

AUXILIARY
FUNCTION
(Irrational)

AUXILIARY
FUNCTION
(Irrational)

INFERIOR FUNCTION
(Rational)

The secondary function is therefore always one whose nature differs from, but is not antagonistic to, the primary function, which means that either of the irrational functions can be auxiliary to one of the rational functions, and vice versa.

Similarly, when sensation is the primary function, intuition cannot be

---

[8] Ibid., par. 667.
[9] Ibid.

the auxiliary function, and vice versa. This is because the effective operation of sensation demands that it focus on sense perceptions in the outer world. This is not compatible with intuition, at least not simultaneously, which "senses" what is happening in the inner world.

Thus thinking and intuition can readily pair, as can thinking and sensation, since the nature of intuition and sensation is not fundamentally opposed to the thinking function. Indeed, either intuition or sensation, both being irrational functions of perception, would be very helpful to the rational judgment of the thinking function.

It is equally true in practice that sensation is bolstered by an auxiliary function of thinking or feeling, feeling is aided by sensation or intuition, and intuition by feeling or thinking.

> The resulting combinations present the familiar picture of, for instance, practical thinking allied with sensation, speculative thinking forging ahead with intuition, artistic intuition selecting and presenting its images with the help of feeling-values, philosophical intuition systematizing its vision into comprehensive thought by means of a powerful intellect, and so on.[10]

The Inferior Function

As already mentioned, those functions other than the one most dominant, most preferred, are relatively subdued. But there is always one function which particularly resists integration into consciousness. This is called the inferior function, or sometimes, to distinguish it from the other inferior functions, "the fourth function." Writes Jung:

> The essence of the inferior function is autonomy: it is independent, it attacks, it fascinates and so spins us about that we are no longer masters of ourselves and can no longer distinguish between ourselves and others.[11]

Marie-Louise von Franz, who worked with Jung for almost thirty years, points out that one of the great problems of the inferior function is that it is generally slow, in contrast with the primary function:

> [That is why] people hate to start work on it; the reaction of the superior function comes out quickly and well adapted, while many people have no

---

[10] Ibid., par. 669.

[11] *Two Essays on Analytical Psychology,* CW 7, par. 85.

idea where their inferior function really is. For instance, thinking types have no idea whether they have feeling or what kind of feeling it is. They have to sit half an hour and meditate as to whether they have feelings about something and, if so, what they are. If you ask a thinking type what he feels, he generally either replies with a thought or gives a quick conventional reaction; and if you then insist on knowing what he really feels, he does not know. Pulling it up from his belly, so to speak, can take half an hour. Or, if an intuitive fills out a tax form he needs a week where other people would take a day.[12]

In Jung's model, as shown in the diagram on page 16, the inferior or fourth function is invariably of the same nature as the primary function: that is to say, when the rational function of thinking is most developed, then the other rational function, feeling, will be inferior; if sensation is dominant, then intuition, the other irrational function, will be the fourth function, and so on.

This accords with general experience: the thinker is regularly tripped up by feeling values; the practical sensation type easily gets into a rut, blind to the possibilities "seen" by intuition; the feeling type is deaf to the conclusions presented by logical thinking; and the intuitive, tuned into the inner world, runs afoul of concrete reality.

One is not necessarily completely oblivious to those perceptions or judgments associated with the inferior function. Thinking types, for example, may know their feelings—insofar as they are capable of introspection[13]—but they do not give them much weight; they will deny their validity and may even claim they are not influenced by them.

Similarly, sensation types who are one-sidedly oriented to physical sense perceptions may have intuitions, but even if they recognize them they tend not to be motivated by them. Feeling types brush away disturbing thoughts, and intuitives simply ignore, or don't notice, what is right in front of their face.

---

[12] *Lectures on Jung's Typology*, p. 8.

[13] The difference between introversion and introspection is that the former refers to the direction in which energy moves, while the latter refers to self-examination. Although the capacity for introspection does seem to be more prevalent among introverts, neither the introverted attitude nor the thinking function has a monopoly on introspection.

Although the inferior function may be conscious as a phenomenon, its true significance nevertheless remains unrecognized. It behaves like many repressed or insufficiently appreciated contents, which are partly conscious and partly unconscious . . . . Thus in normal cases the inferior function remains conscious, at least in its effects; but in a neurosis it sinks wholly or in part into the unconscious.[14]

To the extent that a person functions too one-sidedly, the inferior function becomes correspondingly troublesome, both to oneself and to others. ("Life has no mercy," notes von Franz, "with the inferiority of the inferior function.")[15] The psychic energy claimed by the primary function takes energy away from the inferior function, which falls into the unconscious. There it is prone to be activated in an unnatural way, giving rise to infantile fantasies and a variety of personality disturbances.

This is what regularly happens in a so-called midlife crisis, when an individual has neglected aspects of the personality for so long that they finally demand to be recognized. At such times it is usual to project the cause of the "disturbances" onto others. But only a period of self-reflection and analysis of the fantasies can restore the balance and make further development possible. In fact, as von Franz points out, a crisis of this kind can be a golden opportunity:

> In the realm of the inferior function there is a great concentration of life, so that as soon as the superior function is worn out—begins to rattle and lose oil like an old car—if people succeed in turning to their inferior function, they will rediscover a new potential of life. Everything in the realm of the inferior function becomes exciting, dramatic, full of positive and negative possibilities. There is tremendous tension and the world is, as it were, rediscovered through the inferior function.[16]

—not, however, without some discomfort, for the process of assimilating the inferior function, "raising" it into consciousness, is invariably accompanied by a "lowering" of the superior or primary function.

The thinking type who concentrates on the feeling function, for in-

---

[14] *Psychological Types,* CW 6, par. 764.

[15] *Jung's Typology,* p. 12.

[16] Ibid., p. 11.

stance, has trouble writing an essay, can't think logically; the sensation type trying to develop intuition loses keys, forgets appointments, leaves the stove on overnight; the intuitive becomes fascinated with sound, color, texture, and ignores possibilities; the feeling type burrows into books, immersed in ideas to the detriment of a social life. In each case, the problem becomes one of finding a middle way.

There are typical characteristics associated with each function when it operates in an inferior way. In particular, oversensitivity and strong emotional reactions of any kind—from intense love to blind rage—are a sure sign that the inferior function, along with one or more complexes, has been activated. This naturally gives rise to a multitude of familiar relationship problems.

In therapy, when it becomes desirable or necessary to develop the inferior function, this can only happen gradually and by first going through one of the auxiliary functions. As Jung comments:

> I have frequently observed how an analyst, confronted with a terrific thinking type, for instance, will do his utmost to develop the feeling function directly out of the unconscious. Such an attempt is foredoomed to failure, because it involves too great a violation of the conscious standpoint. Should the violation nevertheless be successful, a really compulsive dependence of the patient on the analyst ensues, a transference that can only be brutally terminated, because, having been left without a standpoint, the patient has made his standpoint the analyst. . . . In order to cushion the impact of the unconscious, an irrational type needs a stronger development of the rational auxiliary function [and vice versa].[17]

The Two Attitude Types

Jung's initial motivation for investigating typology was his need to understand why Freud's view of neurosis was so different from that of Alfred Adler. Freud saw his patients as being preeminently dependent upon, and defining themselves in relation to, significant objects, particularly the parents. Adler's emphasis was on how a person, or subject, seeks security and supremacy. The one supposes that human behavior is

---

[17] *Psychological Types,* CW 6, par. 670.

conditioned by the object, the other finds the determining agency in the subject. Jung expressed appreciation for both points of view:

> The Freudian theory is attractively simple, so much so that it almost pains one if anybody drives in the wedge of a contrary assertion. But the same is true of Adler's theory. It too is of illuminating simplicity and explains as much as the Freudian theory. . . . But how comes it that each investigator sees only one side, and why does each maintain that he has the only valid view? . . . Both are obviously working with the same material; but because of personal peculiarities they each see things from a different angle.[18]

Jung concluded that these "personal peculiarities" were in fact due to typological differences: Freud's system was predominantly extraverted, while Adler's was introverted.

These fundamentally opposite attitude types are found in both sexes and at all levels of society. They are not a matter of conscious choice or inheritance or education. Their occurrence is a general phenomenon having an apparently random distribution. Two children in the same family may even be of opposite types. In fact, Jung believed that one's typological orientation was due to some unconscious, instinctive cause, for which there was likely a biological foundation:

> There are in nature two fundamentally different modes of adaptation which ensure the continued existence of the living organism. . . . The peculiar nature of the extravert constantly urges him to expend and propagate himself in every way, while the tendency of the introvert is to defend himself against all demands from outside, to conserve his energy by withdrawing it from objects, thereby consolidating his own position.[19]

While it is apparent that some individuals have a greater capacity, or disposition, to adapt to life in one way or another, it is not known why. Jung suspected there might be physiological causes of which we have as yet no precise knowledge, since a reversal or distortion of type often proves harmful to one's physical well-being.

No one, of course, is only introverted or extraverted. Although each of us, in the process of following our dominant inclination or adapting to

---

[18] *Two Essays,* CW 7, pars. 56f.
[19] *Psychological Types,* CW 6, par. 559.

our immediate world, invariably develops one attitude more than the other, the opposite attitude is still potentially there. Indeed, family circumstances may force one at an early age to take on an attitude that is not natural, thus violating the person's innate disposition. Notes Jung:

> Whenever such a falsification of type takes place . . . the individual becomes neurotic later, and can be cured only by developing the attitude consonant with his nature.[20]

This certainly complicates the type issue, since everyone is more or less neurotic—that is, one-sided.

In general, the introvert is simply unconscious of his or her extraverted side, because of an habitual orientation toward the inner world. The extravert's introversion is similarly dormant, waiting to emerge. The undeveloped attitude becomes an aspect of the shadow, all those things about ourselves we are not conscious of, our unrealized potential, our "unlived life." Moreover, being unconscious, when the inferior attitude surfaces—that is, when the introvert's extraversion, or the extravert's introversion, is activated—it will tend to emerge, just like the inferior function, in an emotional, socially unadapted way.

Since what is of value to the introvert is the opposite of what is important to the extravert, the inferior attitude regularly bedevils relationships. To illustrate this, Jung tells the story of two youths, one an introverted type, the other extraverted, rambling in the countryside.[21] They come upon a castle. Both want to visit it, but for different reasons. The introvert wonders what it's like inside; the extravert is game for adventure.

At the gate the introvert draws back. "Perhaps we aren't allowed in," he says—imagining guard dogs, policemen and fines in the background. The extravert is undeterred. "Oh, they'll let us in all right," he says—with visions of kindly old watchmen and the possibility of meeting an attractive girl.

On the strength of extraverted optimism, the two finally get inside the castle. There they find some dusty rooms with a collection of old manuscripts. As it happens, such things are the main interest of the introvert.

---

[20] Ibid., par. 560.
[21] See *Two Essays*, CW 7, pars. 81ff.

He whoops with joy and enthusiastically peruses the treasures. He talks to the caretaker, asks for the curator, becomes quite animated; his shyness has vanished, objects have taken on a seductive glamour.

Meanwhile, the spirits of the extravert have fallen. He becomes glum, begins to yawn. There are no kindly watchmen, no pretty girls, just an old castle made into a museum. The manuscripts remind him of a library; library is associated with university, university with studies and examinations. He finds the whole thing incredibly boring.

"Isn't it marvelous," cries the introvert, "look at these!"—to which the extravert replies grumpily, "Nothing here for me, let's go." This annoys the introvert, who secretly swears never again to go rambling with an inconsiderate extravert. Meanwhile, the latter is completely frustrated and now can think of nothing but that he'd rather be out of doors on a lovely spring day.

Jung points out that the two youths are wandering together in happy symbiosis until they come upon the castle. They enjoy a degree of harmony because they are collectively adapted to each other; the natural attitude of the one complements the natural attitude of the other.

The introvert is curious but hesitant; the extravert opens the door. But once inside, the types invert themselves: the former becomes fascinated by the object, the latter by his negative thoughts. The introvert now cannot be induced to go out and the extravert regrets ever setting foot in the castle.

What has happened? The introvert has become extraverted and the extravert introverted. But the opposite attitude of each manifests in a socially inferior way: the introvert, overpowered by the object, doesn't appreciate that his friend is bored; the extravert, disappointed in his expectations of romantic adventure, becomes moody and sullen, and doesn't care about his friend's excitement.

This is a simple example of the way in which the inferior attitude is autonomous. What we are not conscious of in ourselves is by definition beyond our control. When the undeveloped attitude is constellated, we are prey to all kinds of disruptive emotions—we are "complexed."

In the course of life, we are generally obliged to develop both introversion and extraversion to some extent. This is necessary not only in order to coexist with others, both in close relationships and in our working life, but also for the development of individual character. We cannot in the long run allow one part of our personality to be cared for symbiotically by another. Yet that is in effect what happens when we rely on friends, relatives or lovers to carry our inferior attitude or function.

If the inferior attitude is not consciously allowed some expression in our lives, we are likely to become bored and boring, uninteresting to both ourselves and others. And since there is energy tied up with whatever in ourselves is unconscious, we will not have the zest for life that goes with a well-balanced personality.

It is important to realize that one's activities are not always a reliable indication of one's attitude type. The person hailed as the life of the party may indeed be an extravert, but not necessarily. Similarly, long periods of solitude do not automatically mean that one is an introvert. The party-goer may be an introvert living out his or her shadow; the solitaire may be an extravert who has simply run out of steam or been forced by circumstances to be alone. In other words, while a particular activity may be associated with introversion or extraversion, this does not so easily translate into which type one is.

The crucial factor in determining type, as opposed to simply which attitude is currently prominent, is therefore not what one does but rather the motivation for doing it—*the direction in which one's energy naturally, and usually, flows:* for the extravert the object is interesting and attractive, while inner reality is more important to the introvert.

The Role of the Unconscious

There is a simple elegance and symmetry to Jung's model of typology, but its use as a diagnostic tool, or even as a guide to self-understanding, is far from simple. Thus, although Jung did not foresee the commercial use of his model, he did warn against its misuse as "a practical guide to a good judgment of human character."[22]

---

[22] *Psychological Types,* CW 6, preface, pp. xivf. Among the widely used type tests based on Jungian principles is the Myers-Briggs Type Indicator (MBTI).

Whether one is predominantly introverted or extraverted, there are inescapable psychological implications due to the role of the unconscious. In short, the great difficulty in diagnosing the types is due to the fact that the dominant conscious attitude is unconsciously compensated or balanced by its opposite.

Introversion or extraversion, as a typical attitude, indicates an essential bias that conditions one's whole psychic process. The habitual mode of reaction determines not only the style of behavior, but also the quality of subjective experience. Moreover, it determines what is required in terms of compensation by the unconscious. Since either attitude is by itself one-sided, there would be a complete loss of psychic balance if there were no compensation by an unconscious counterposition. Hence alongside or behind the introvert's usual way of functioning there is an unconscious extraverted attitude, and, similarly, the one-sidedness of extraversion is mitigated by an unconscious introverted attitude.

Strictly speaking, there is no demonstrable "attitude of the unconscious," but only ways of functioning that are colored by unconsciousness. It is in this sense that one can speak of a compensating attitude in the unconscious.

As we have seen, generally only one of the four functions is differentiated enough to be freely manipulable by the conscious will. The others are wholly or partially unconscious, and the inferior function mostly so. Thus the conscious orientation of the thinking type is balanced by unconscious feeling, and vice versa, while sensation is compensated by intuition, and so on.

Jung speaks of a "numinal accent" that falls either on the object or on the subject, depending on whether one is extraverted or introverted.[23] This numinal accent also "selects" one or other of the four functions, whose differentiation is essentially an empirical consequence of typical differences in the functional attitude. Thus one finds extraverted feeling in an introverted intellectual, introverted sensation in an extraverted intuitive, and so on.

An additional problem in establishing a person's typology is that un-

---

[23] Ibid., pars. 982ff.

conscious, undifferentiated functions can color a personality to such an extent that an outside observer might easily mistake one type for another. For instance, the rational types (thinking and feeling) will have relatively inferior irrational functions (sensation and intuition); what they consciously and intentionally do may accord with reason (from their own point of view), but what happens to them may well be characterized by primitive sensations and intuitions. As Jung points out,

> Since there are vast numbers of people whose lives consist more of what happens to them than of actions governed by rational intentions, [an on-looker], after observing them closely, might easily describe [thinking and feeling types] as irrational. And one has to admit that only too often a man's unconscious makes a far stronger impression on an observer than his consciousness does, and that his actions are of considerably more importance than his rational intentions.[24]

It can be as difficult to establish one's own type as that of another person, especially when people have already become bored with their primary function and dominant attitude. Von Franz comments:

> They very often assure you with absolute sincerity that they belong to the type opposite from what they really are. The extravert swears that he is deeply introverted, and vice versa. This comes from the fact that the inferior function subjectively feels itself to be the real one; it feels itself the more important, more genuine attitude. . . . It does no good, therefore, to think of what *matters* most when trying to discover one's type; rather ask: "What do I habitually *do* most?"[25]

In practice, it is often helpful to ask oneself: What is my greatest cross? From what do I suffer the most? Where is it in life that I always knock my head against the wall and feel foolish? In what situations do I find my foot in my mouth? And further afield: what is there about me that friends and relatives constantly complain about?

The answers to such questions generally lead to the inferior attitude and function, which then, with some determination and a good dose of patience, may perhaps be brought to a degree of consciousness.

---

[24] Ibid., par. 602.
[25] *Jung's Typology,* p. 16.

Typology, Persona and Shadow

Jung's model of typology, when used responsibly, is a valuable guide to our dominant psychological disposition, the way we mostly are. It also reveals, by inference, the way we mostly aren't—but could also be.

Where, then, is the rest of us (mostly)?

Theoretically, we can say that the inferior or undeveloped attitude and functions are part of that side of ourselves Jung called the shadow. The reason for this is both conceptual and pragmatic.

Conceptually, the shadow, like the ego, is a complex, an agglomeration of associations. But where the ego, as the dominant complex of consciousness, is associated with aspects of oneself that are more or less known (as "I"), the shadow consists of personality characteristics that are not part of one's usual way of being in the world, and therefore are more or less alien to one's sense of personal identity.

The shadow is potentially both creative and destructive: creative in that it represents aspects of oneself that have been buried or that might yet be realized; destructive in the sense that its value system and motivations tend to undermine or disturb one's conscious image of oneself.

Everything that is not ego is relatively unconscious; hence before the contents of the unconscious have been differentiated, the shadow *is,* in effect, the unconscious. Since the opposite attitude and the inferior functions are by definition relatively unconscious, they are naturally tied up with the shadow.

In one's immediate world, there are attitudes and behavior that are socially acceptable, and those that are not. In our formative years it is natural to repress, or suppress, the unacceptable aspects of ourselves. They "fall into" the unconscious and become shadow. What is left is the persona—the "I" one presents to the outside world.

The persona would live up to what is expected, what is proper. It is both a useful bridge socially and an indispensable protective covering; without a persona, we are simply too vulnerable. We regularly cover up our inferiorities with a persona, since we do not like our weaknesses to be seen. Civilized society depends on interactions between people through the persona. But it is psychologically unhealthy to identify with it, to believe we are "nothing but" the person we show to others.

Generally speaking, the shadow is less civilized, more primitive, cares little for social propriety. What is of value to the persona is anathema to the shadow, and vice versa. Hence the shadow and the persona function in a compensatory way: the brighter the light, the darker the shadow. The more one identifies with the persona—which in effect is to deny that one has a shadow—the more trouble one will have with the unacknowledged "other side" of the personality.

Thus the shadow constantly challenges the morality of the persona, and, to the extent that ego-consciousness identifies with the persona, the shadow also threatens the ego. In the process of psychological development that Jung called individuation, disidentification from the persona and the conscious assimilation of the shadow go hand in hand. The ideal is to have an ego strong enough to acknowledge both the persona and the shadow without identifying with either.

This is not as easy as it sounds. We tend to identify with what we are good at, and why shouldn't we? The superior function, after all, has an undeniable utilitarian value. It greases the wheels of life and generally brings praise, material rewards and a good degree of satisfaction. Thus it inevitably becomes a prominent aspect of the persona. Why give it up? The answer is that we don't or won't—unless we have to. And when do we "have to"?—when we encounter situations in life that are not amenable to the way we usually function.

In practice, as noted earlier, the shadow and everything associated with it is virtually synonomous with unlived life. "There must be more to life than this," is a remark heard often in the analyst's office. All that I consciously am and aspire to be effectively shuts out what I might be, could be, *also am*. Some of "what I also am" has been repressed because it was or is unacceptable to oneself or others, and some is simply unrealized potential.

Through introspection, we can become aware of shadow aspects of the personality, but we may still resist them or fear their influence. And even where they are known and would be welcome, they are not readily available to the conscious will. For instance, my intuition may be shadowy—primitive and unadapted—so I cannot call it up when it's needed. I may know that feeling is required in a particular situation but for the life of me can't muster it. I want to enjoy the party but my carefree extraverted side has vanished. I may know I'm due for some introversion, but the lure of the bright lights is just too strong.

The shadow does not necessarily demand equal time with the ego, but for a balanced personality it does require recognition. For the introvert this may involve an occasional night on the town—against her "better judgment." For the extravert it might involve—in spite of himself—an evening staring at the wall.

In general, the person whose shadow is dormant gives the impression of being dull and stodgy. This is true no matter which attitude is dominant: the extravert seems to lack depth; the introvert appears socially inept, lifeless.

The introvert's psychological situation is laid bare in the writer Franz Kafka's observation:

> Whoever leads a solitary life, and yet now and then wants to attach himself somewhere; whoever, according to changes in the time of day, the weather, the state of his business and the like, suddenly wishes to see any arm at all to which he might cling—he will not be able to manage for long without a window looking on to the street.[26]

Similarly, the extravert may only become conscious of his or her shadow when struck by the vacuity of social intercourse.

There is a balance between introversion and extraversion, as there is between the normally opposing functions, but it rarely becomes necessary—or even possible—to seek it out, until and unless the conscious ego-personality falls on its face. In that case, which happily manifests as a nervous breakdown rather than a more serious psychotic break, the shadow side demands to be recognized. The resulting turmoil, as we will see in chapter 3 of this book, is not entirely negative, for it has the advantage of overcoming the tyranny of the dominant attitude of consciousness. If the symptoms are then attended to with some seriousness, the whole personality can be enlivened.

---

[26] "The Street Window," in *The Penal Colony,* p. 39.

There is by definition a natural conflict between ego and shadow, but when one has made a commitment to live out as much of one's potential as possible, then the integration of the shadow—including the inferior attitude and functions—evolves from being merely theoretically desirable to becoming a practical necessity. Hence the process of assimilating the shadow requires the capacity to live with some psychological tension.

The introverted man, for instance, under the influence of his inferior extraverted shadow, is prone to imagine he is missing something: vivacious women, fast company, excitement. He himself may see these as chimeras, but his shadow yearns for them. His shadow will lead him into the darkest venues, and then, as often as not, whimsically abandon him. What is left? A lonely introvert who longs for home.

On top of that, the extraverting introvert who is taken at face value—as a true extravert—is liable to end up in hot water. Whereas the introverting extravert has only himself to deal with, the extraverting introvert often makes a tremendous impact on those who cross his path, but he might not want to be with them the next day. When his introversion reasserts itself, he may literally want nothing to do with other people. Thus the introverted thinking type whose shadow is a carefree Don Juan, say, wreaks havoc on the unsuspecting hearts of others.

True extraverts genuinely enjoy being part of the crowd. That is their natural home. They are restless alone, not because they are avoiding themselves, but because they have few parameters for establishing their identity outside of the group. The introverted shadow of extraverts encourages them to stay home and find out who they are. But just as introverts may be abandoned by their shadows in a noisy bar, so extraverts may be left high and dry—feeling very lonely—when on their own.

The opposite attitude and the inferior functions are commonly personified as shadow figures in dreams and fantasies. Dream activity becomes heightened when a function not usually available to consciousness is required. Thus a man who is a thinking type, after a quarrel with his mate, for instance, may be assailed in his dreams by images of primitive feeling persons, dramatically illustrating a side of himself still unassimilated. Similarly, the sensation type stuck in a rut may be confronted in dreams by an intuitive friend showing new possibilities.

To assimilate or develop a function means to live with it in the fore-ground of consciousness. A minor sop is not enough. For instance, von Franz writes, "if [an intuitive] does a little cooking or sewing, it does not mean that the sensation function has been assimilated":

Assimilation means that the whole adaptation of conscious life, for a while, lies on that one function. Switching over to an auxiliary function takes place when one feels that the present way of living has become life-less, when one gets more or less constantly bored with oneself and one's activities. . . . The best way to know how to switch is simply to say, "All right, all this does not mean anything to me any more. Where in my past life is an activity that I feel I could still enjoy? An activity out of which I could still get a kick?" If a person then genuinely picks up that activity, he will see that he has switched over to another function.[27]

—and, to some extent, assimilated an aspect of the shadow.

A Dinner Party with the Types

The following scenario illustrates in a light vein how Jung's model of ty-pology might look in everyday life.[28]

The Extraverted Feeling Type

Our hostess is a feeling type. Who else would go to the trouble of bring-ing this group together? Even the invitations—elegantly handwritten on beautiful stationery—express her joy at entertaining these dear friends.

She is a charming woman, warm and voluptuous as a Renoir painting, a marvelous housekeeper, open minded, obliging, worldly. She is very attractive and hospitable, offering fine food beautifully prepared and pre-sented. Her home shows great taste.

Since she tends to repeat the opinions of her husband and father, her conversation is not particularly exciting. Sometimes her views are those of religious leaders or other well-known personalities in her community. In all cases she expresses them with the greatest conviction, as if they originated with her. She does not realize that her only real contribution to

---

[27] *Jung's Typology,* p. 59.
[28] Originally published in German in Sammlung Dalp, *Handschriften-deutung* (The In-terpretation of Handwriting). Adapted by Vicki Cowan.

the evening—other than the food—is the emotional tone associated with what she says.

She married a connoisseur—an aesthete—who puts great value on living a life of unobtrusive luxury.

The Introverted Sensation Type

Our host is an art historian and collector. But thinking is for him an inferior function, so although he collects books and owns an impressive collection, he does not delve deeply into their content.

He is tall, dark and lean, as silent as his wife is talkative. He seems to barricade himself behind his wife's chatter. He cannot fathom her dedication to these dinner parties which force him to abandon his beautiful, quiet study. However, they have agreed that she will organize the social side of their life and he knows from long experience that she is a master at the art of entertaining. She is the one who brings needed extraversion to their marriage and connects them to the outside world.

He greets his guests in an elegant way, a bit restrained, and offers his slender hand to the well-known lawyer just coming in. In fact, he despises this woman, who is an extraverted thinking type. In greeting her, he mistakenly says, "Good-bye." The hostess, who observes this gaffe with horror, tries to make up for it with a double dose of friendliness.

The Extraverted Thinking Type

The lawyer is the first guest to arrive. Being very concerned with her social position, she would never forgive herself if she were late.

Having recently graduated with honors, she is at the beginning of a promising career. Already she has achieved considerable status as a speaker. Her judgment is accurate and her logic indisputable. Her arguments are based on accepted, concrete facts, speculative ideas being alien to her. As with most extraverted thinking types, she is conservative and places great importance on objective data. Since her auxiliary function is sensation, she is also practical and well organized in both her personal and professional life.

Of her true feelings we know very little. It is said that eventually she will marry the boss's son.

The Extraverted Sensation Type

Two new guests arrive—a leading industrialist and his wife. He is an extraverted sensation type with auxiliary thinking. His wife is an introverted feeling type with intuition as an auxiliary function. This couple illustrates how individuals with opposite dominant functions often attract and complement each other.[29]

The industrialist has good common sense, a positive work ethic and a practical, enterprising nature. He knows how to handle himself in any situation. An intelligent and authoritative executive, he leads a whole army of employees and yet finds time to oversee every detail. It is rather astonishing to observe what he accomplishes professionally and socially in the course of a single day.

Nevertheless, at times he lacks a broad viewpoint. He lives so entirely in the moment that he cannot predict the results of his actions. Because his intuition remains undeveloped, he comprehends only what has already occurred and cannot foresee possible future dangers.

He is well dressed but lacks refinement, being loud and tactless. He seems warmhearted but is overwhelming as well. At dinner he is greedy.

None of their acquaintances understands what keeps him and his wife together. Nor does he; he only knows that from the moment he met her he was entranced, and that he could not live without her.

The Introverted Feeling Type

This woman, the industrialist's wife, is quiet and impenetrable. Her eyes have a mysterious depth. An inexhaustible topic of conversation for the hostess, who loves to analyze the relationships of others, is the powerful influence this young woman has over her husband.

This small and fragile woman seemingly does nothing to excite the amazing dependency of this heavy and insensitive man. Yet he follows her everywhere with his eyes and tries to catch hers. He asks her opinion constantly.

The explanation lies in the complementary nature of these opposite

---

[29] In this case, the dominant function of the man is actually opposite to the woman's secondary function.

types. For this man, his wife is the bearer of those introverted depths to which he has no access within himself. For this reason she personifies the image he carries of the ideal feminine—his anima.

Introverted feeling types do not express their emotions often, but when they do it is with great power. These individuals accumulate an enormous amount of inner affect and this compressed intensity lends them a special aura, often perceived as an inviolate and mysterious strength. Such types are often artistically gifted. This young woman has one real passion in her life—music. For her, music expresses the world of her feeling in a pure and uninterrupted form. Here she finds complete harmony uncontaminated by the worldly reality she finds so jarring.

Without her husband, however, she would have little contact with the outside world. Clearly he personifies her inner image of the masculine—her animus.

The Introverted Thinking Type

In the meantime, a new visitor has come in. He is a professor of medicine, specializing in sleeping sickness. He is as well known for his boring lectures as for his new discoveries in his field. He has no contact with his students and dislikes sharing his ideas. Even his patients do not interest him, being nothing more than "cases" which he needs in order to pursue his research.

His handwriting is very small with a peculiar way of connecting the letters, readable only by himself and his assistant. It gives the impression of an impenetrable weaving. A despairing student once said, "This is not writing, this is knitting!"

One never sees the professor with his wife (who incidentally is an extraverted feeling type, his typological opposite). They never go out together and rumor has it that she is totally uneducated and was once his cleaning lady.

The Extraverted Intuitive Type

The last guest comes rushing in from the airport. He is an engineer, bubbling over with new ideas, drunk with their possibilities. But he is unlikely to put these ideas into action; instead, he will probably inspire others to do so. At table, he talks enthusiastically about new travel plans, which seem over-adventurous to the host, and gobbles down his food without stopping to notice it.

The other guests are noticeably uncomfortable around this charismatic young man. He seems to be unrelated to the reality of the world they live in, but at the same time his ideas are intriguing and seductive.

The Introverted Intuitive Type

One place-setting at the table is empty—the space for the poor young poet. He neither came nor offered an explanation; he simply forgot he was invited. He is a skinny young man with a fine oval face and wide, dreamy eyes.

That evening he was absorbed totally in his manuscript. Stimulated finally by hunger pangs, he went to his usual cheap restaurant. Since he has no feeling for time and space, he arrived late. (It had taken him half an hour to find his glasses.) It did not bother him that the food was mediocre. He ate his meal in an abstracted way, glancing now and then at the newspaper beside his plate.

After dinner, he went for a long walk under the starry sky, not realizing till too late that he had left his overcoat at the restaurant. Strolling along he was unaccountably inspired to create a poem—a sonnet filled with metaphysical wonders. And he was overwhelmed with joy.

All of a sudden he remembered the invitation to the dinner party. But it was now too late. This error, or lapse, reflected his unacknowledged feelings exactly. Though the introvert fears life's demands, there is also a touch of secret haughtiness mixed in with the shyness.

He thinks, "I shall send the lady my poem, the best I have to give." But will he really do so, or just think about it? And if he does, will the hostess understand? Yet this poor poet, comical and grotesque in his shortsightedness—this fool, who shies away from the joy and conflicts of society—may have given birth to a poem of universal resonance.

The Group

The conversation over dinner becomes quite animated. Politics, theater, sensational court cases, books and films are all discussed. The two extraverts, the lawyer and the industrialist, become involved in a heated debate and only their manners prevent them from comng to blows.

The professor is silent. Large parties make him feel slow and awkward, and he does not enjoy the sophisticated surroundings. But at the end of the meal, against his own good judgment, he suddenly speaks up. What does he talk about? His hobby, which happens to be sleeping sickness! But since his feeling function is undeveloped and childlike, he does not realize the reactions of the other guests, nor does he sense his own inappropriateness.

The others respond in various ways to the professor's discourse, each for a different reason. The lawyer is always curious about noteworthy or educational ideas; the industrialist is most interested in what the professor says about the practical implementation of his work; the refined host is nauseated by the graphic description of the illness and his delicate digestion is upset.

But the most profound reaction is experienced by the hostess. She had tried at the beginning, unsuccessfully, to channel the professor's long monologue into a different direction. Eventually, unable to follow the conversation, she gave up. She cannot comprehend such conversation and finds it vaguely offensive. Her happy face has fallen, her eyelids are heavy and she is bored to death. Only at the end of the party, showing off her home and children to the industrialist's wife, does she regain her lively nature and happy disposition.

2
Getting To Know Yourself

When an inner situation is not made conscious,
it happens outside, as fate.
—C.G. Jung.

Archetypes and Complexes

Wrestling with your typological orientation is a good start in understanding who you are. But it is child's play compared to becoming acquainted with your complexes.

Complexes are normal and present in everyone; they are the building blocks of the personality. Just as atoms and molecules are the invisible components of physical objects, so complexes are the hidden parts of ourselves; they comprise our identity and are what makes us tick.

When I first went into analysis I knew nothing about complexes. I had heard the word, usually in a pejorative context, but I did not know what it meant. I had read about the Oedipus complex, which seemed to have something to do with a man's unconscious desire to kill his father so he could have his mother all to himself. Well, that was Freud.

Immersing myself in Jung, I learned that complexes are essentially feeling-toned ideas that over the years accumulate around certain images, for instance those of "mother," "father," "money," "power" and so on. I also learned that they have a so-called archetypal core: behind emotional associations with the personal mother, say, there is the archetype of the mother—an age-old collective image spanning the opposites, from nourishment and security ("positive" mother) to devouring possessiveness ("negative" mother).

The notion of archetypes was puzzling until I absorbed the following:

[Archetypes] are, indeed, an instinctive *trend,* as marked as the impulse of birds to build nests, or ants to form organized colonies.[30]

---

[30] Jung, "Approaching the Unconscious," *Man and His Symbols,* p. 69.

Archetypes are systems of readiness for action, and at the same time images and emotions. They are inherited with the brain structure—indeed they are its psychic aspect.[31]

It is not . . . a question of inherited *ideas* but of inherited *possibilities* of ideas. Nor are they individual acquisitions but, in the main, common to all, as can be seen from [their] universal occurrence.[32]

Archetypes . . . present themselves *as ideas and images,* like everything else that becomes a content of consciousness.[33]

Jung used the simile of the spectrum to illustrate the difference between instinct and the archetype as an "instinctual image":

The dynamism of instinct is lodged as it were in the infra-red part of the spectrum, whereas the instinctual image lies in the ultra-violet part. . . . The realization and assimilation of instinct never take place at the red end, i.e., by absorption into the instinctual sphere, but only through integration of the image which signifies and at the same time evokes the instinct.[34]

INSTINCTS	ARCHETYPES
infrared ———————————————————— ultraviolet	
(**Physiological:** body symptoms, instinctual perceptions, etc.)	(**Psychological:** spirit, dreams, conceptions, images, fantasies, etc.)

So, an archetype is a primordial, structural element of the human psyche, an instinctive, universal tendency to form certain ideas and images and to behave in certain ways. I could follow that. However, I still did not connect complexes with my own life and what they had to do with me finding myself on my knees. Then I did Jung's Word Association Experiment, a "test" he developed to illustrate how unconscious factors can disturb the workings of consciousness.

In the Word Association Experiment there is a list of a hundred words,

---

[31] "Mind and Earth," *Civiliaztion in Transition,* CW 10, par. 53.
[32] "Concerning the Archetypes and the Anima Concept," *The Archetypes and the Collective Unconscious,* CW 9i, par. 136.
[33] "On the Nature of the Psyche," *The Structure and Dynamics of the Psyche,* CW 8, par. 435.
[34] Ibid., par. 414.

to each of which you are asked to respond with what first comes into your head. The delay in responding (the response time) is measured with a stop watch, as for instance:

"Head"— "bed" (0.8 sec.)
"Marry"— "together" (1.7 sec.)
"Woman"— "friend" (2 sec.)
"Home"—(long pause) "none" (5.6 sec.)

—and so on.

Then you go through the list a second time, noting different responses to the same words. Finally you are asked for comments on those words to which you had a longer-than-average response time, a merely mechanical response or a different association on the second run-through; all these had been flagged by the questioner as "complex indicators."

It was an illuminating experience. It was also deflating. It convinced me that complexes were not only real but were alive in me and quite autonomous, independent of my will. I realized they could affect my memory, my thoughts, my moods, my behavior. I was not free to be me—there *was* no "me"—when I was in the grip of a complex.

Freud described dreams as the *via regia* to the unconscious; Jung showed that the royal road to the unconscious is rather the complex, the architect of both dreams and symptoms. In fact, Jung originally gave the name "complex psychology" to his school of thought, to distinguish it from Freud's school of psychoanalysis.

The activation of a complex is always marked by the presence of some strong emotion, whether it be love, hate, rage, sadness or joy. Everyone is complexed by something, which is to say, we all react emotionally when the right buttons are pushed. Or, to put it another way, an emotional reaction *means* that a complex has been constellated. When we are emotional we can't think straight and hardly know how we feel. We speak and act out of the complex, and when it has run its course we wonder what took over.

We cannot get rid of our complexes because they are deeply rooted in our personal history. Complexes are part and parcel of who we are. The most we can do is become aware of how we are influenced by them and how they interfere with our conscious intentions. As long as we are unconscious of our complexes, we are prone to being overwhelmed or driven by them. When we understand them, they lose their power to affect us. They do not disappear but over time their grip may loosen.

Life would be very dull without complexes. They are the very stuff of history and drama, films, novels and TV sitcoms. On the personal level they can either spice our relationships, or poison them with resentment, irritation, self-pity, anxiety, fear and guilt.

A complex is a bundle of associations, sometimes painful, sometimes joyful, always accompanied by affect. It has energy and a life of its own. It can upset digestion, breathing and the rate at which the heart beats. It behaves like a partial personality. When you want to say or do something and a complex interferes, you find yourself saying or doing something quite different from what you intended. Your best intentions are upset, exactly as if you had been interfered with by another person.

In some conditions, schizophrenia for example, complexes emancipate themselves from conscious control to such an extent that they can become visible and audible. They appear as visions and speak in voices that are like those of definite people. But this is not in itself pathological. Complexes are regularly personified in dreams, and one can train oneself so they become visible or audible also in a waking condition. It is even psychologically healthy to do so, for when you give them a voice, a face, a personality, they are less likely to take over when you're not looking.

We like to think we are masters in our own house, but clearly we are not. We are renters at best. Psychologically we live in a boarding house of saints and knaves, nobles and villains, run by a landlord who for all we know is indifferent to the lot. We fancy we can do what we want, but when it comes to a showdown our will is hampered by fellow boarders with a mind of their own.

To sum up: complexes have a tendency to live their own lives in spite of our conscious intentions. Both our personal unconscious and the collective unconscious consist of an unknown number of these fragmentary personalities. This actually explains a lot that is otherwise quite puzzling, like the fact that one is able to dramatize mental contents. When someone creates a character on the stage, or in a poem or novel, it is not simply a product of that person's imagination. Writers may deny that their work has a psychological meaning, but in fact you can read their mind when you study the characters they create.

Marie-Louise von Franz once told me of a man who after two years of bringing his dreams for analysis confessed that he had made them all up. "The joke's on you," she said. "Where do you think they came from? You said what was in you. That's as real as any dream."

Jung saw complexes as islands of consciousness split off from the ego-mainland. This is a useful metaphor. When you're emotional, caught in a complex, you're cut off from rational ego resources; the complex rules the personality for as long as you stay on the island. When the storm dies down you swim ashore and lick your wounds, wondering what on earth got into you.

More about Persona

As a young man I was caught up in the idea of myself as a struggling writer. That was my persona, the way I thought of myself and how I presented myself to others. I could not imagine life without this image of myself. More accurately, I did not exist outside of it. And so for many years I typed away in a small shed at the foot of the garden, identifying with every other struggling writer who had ever lived. I was disappointed that no one would publish what I wrote, but at the same time I secretly exulted, anticipating the day when I would be discovered.

Jung describes the persona as an aspect of the collective psyche, which means there is nothing individual about it. It may *feel* individual— quite special and unique, in fact—but such designations as "struggling writer," "father," "teacher," "doctor" and so on are on the one hand simply social identities, and on the other ideal images. They do not describe a particular person; they do not distinguish one doctor or father or teacher or writer from any other.

Like any other complex, one's persona has certain attributes and behavior patterns associated with it, as well as collective expectations to live up to: a struggling writer, for instance, is a serious thinker, on the brink of recognition; a teacher is a figure of authority, dedicated to imparting knowledge; a doctor is wise, versed in the arcane mysteries of the body; a priest is close to God, morally impeccable; a mother loves her children and would sacrifice her life for them; an accountant knows his figures but is unemotional, and so on.

That is why we experience a sense of shock when we read of a teacher accused of molesting a student, a doctor charged with drug abuse, an adulterous priest, a mother who drowns her child, or an accountant who fiddles the books to pay gambling debts.

The development of a collectively suitable persona always involves a compromise between what we know ourselves to be and what is expected of us, such as a degree of courtesy and innocuous behavior. There is nothing intrinsically wrong with that. In Greek, the word *persona* meant a mask worn by actors to indicate the role they played. On this level, it is an asset in mixing with other people. It is also useful as a protective covering. Close friends may know us for what we are; the rest of the world knows only what we choose to show them. Indeed, without an outer layer of some kind, we are simply too vulnerable. Only the foolish and naive attempt to move through life without a persona.

However, we must be able to drop our persona in situations where it is not appropriate. This is especially true in intimate relationships. There is a difference between myself as an analyst and who I am when I'm not practicing. The doctor's skill at heart surgery is little comfort to a neglected mate. The teacher's knowledge does not impress her teenage son who wants to borrow the car. The wise preacher leaves his collar and his rhetoric at home when he goes courting.

By handsomely rewarding the persona, the outside world invites us to identify with it. Money, respect and power come to those who can perform single-mindedly and well in a social role. No wonder we can forget that our essential identity is something other than the work we do, or our function in the collective. From being a useful convenience, therefore, the persona easily becomes a trap. It is one thing to realize this, quite another to do something about it.

The poet Rainer Maria Rilke put it quite well:

We discover, indeed, that we do not know our part; we look for a mirror; we want to rub off the paint, to remove all that is artificial and become real. But somewhere a bit of mummery that we forget still sticks to us. A trace of exaggeration remains in our eyebrows; we do not notice that the corners of our lips are twisted. And thus we go about, a laughing-stock, a mere half-thing: neither real beings nor actors.[35]

Identification with a social role is a frequent source of midlife crisis, because it inhibits our adaptation to a given situation beyond what is collectively prescribed. Who am I without a mask? Is there anybody home? I am a prominent and respected member of the community. Why, then, is my wife more interested in somebody else?

We cannot get rid of ourselves in favor of a collective identity without some consequences: we lose sight of who we are without our protective covering; our reactions are predetermined by collective expectations (we do and think and feel what our persona "should" do, think and feel); those close to us complain of our emotional distance; and, worst of all, we cannot imagine life without it.

Many married people have a joint persona as "a happy couple." Whatever may be happening between them, they greet the world with a united front. They are perfectly matched, the envy of their friends. What is going on behind the curtains is anybody's guess.

More about Shadow

When I first started analysis, shadow was just a word to me, an interesting concept. I had read *Dr. Jekyll and Mr. Hyde*. I had seen *The Secret Life of Walter Mitty*. True, it seemed to explain much about human nature that was otherwise a mystery, but I can't say I understood what was meant by the term psychologically.

One evening I went to a dinner party to celebrate a friend's opening at a prestigious art gallery. About two dozen friends of the artist sat down to a banquet at a long table. There were five courses and a vintage wine with each. I was seated opposite a middle-aged woman who talked at me nonstop through the soup. She had an opinion about everything, which

---

[35] *The Notebook of Malte Laurids Brigge*, p. 217.

she delivered in a high-pitched, grating voice.

Midway through the salad I suddenly stood up and dumped my bowl on her head. Lettuce and tomatoes and chives and cucumbers and a tasty oil and vinegar dressing ran down her hair and dribbled into her lap.

She was shocked; I was mortified. Fortunately her husband had a sense of humor, because she didn't.

That very afternoon I had been talking to my analyst about Jung's description of the shadow, specifically the notion that a mild-mannered person must be sitting on a lot of repressed aggression.

"Well, there's no aggression in me," I laughed. "I never get upset about anything."

It was true. I was the perfect gentleman, always polite and accommodating. I could not remember ever being angry at anyone. Oh, occasionally I felt some irritation, but that was well under control. I suggested to my analyst that over the years I must have integrated my shadow very well. He just smiled.

The next time I saw him I was more humble. "I can't think what got into me," I shrugged.

"It's really quite simple," said my analyst. "Your shadow had just had enough."

Recently a friend of mine was asked to toast the bride at his niece's wedding. He liked the man she was marrying, but to me he confessed that he couldn't see why she did. She was pretty conventional and he was anything but. He was a high school drop-out and had never had a steady job; he spent his time in pubs dealing dope and planning his next big score. He was a charming con-man, said my friend; he lived on the edge—"but what can you do, he's her choice."

The wedding was a posh affair at a local golf club. My friend rented a tux and had his brief speech ready. When it came his turn, after a few drinks, he said the usual things about what she was like when she was little and oh my, wasn't she something now. And then, out of the blue, he found himself saying not very nice things about the groom—that he was an ill-disguised thug, a king-pin in the local drug trade, that his fondest wish was to have a wife who could support him, and on and on.

He made a joke of all this, but the groom's parents were completely spooked. The bride let it pass and her new husband was too drunk to notice, but my friend couldn't sleep that night. How could he, always concerned to do the right thing, do just the opposite?

The answer lies in his shadow. Where he was concerned to put on a good front, as most of us are, his shadow was not.

As noted in the previous chapter, everything about ourselves that we are not conscious of is shadow. Psychologically, the shadow opposes and compensates the conscious ego-personality. The realization of how and when it enters our life is a precondition for self-knowledge. The more we become conscious of our shadow, the less of a threat it is—and the more psychologically substantial we become.

In Jung's description, the shadow, or at least its dark side, is composed of morally inferior wishes and motives, childish fantasies and resentments, etc.—all those things about ourselves we are not proud of and regularly seek to hide from others. In civilized societies aggression is a prominent aspect of the shadow, simply because it is not socially acceptable; it is nipped in the bud in childhood and its expression in adult life is met with heavy sanctions.

By and large, then, the shadow is a hodge-podge of repressed desires and uncivilized impulses. It is possible to become conscious of these, but in the meantime they are projected onto others. Just as we may mistake a real man or woman for the soul-mate we yearn for, so we see our devils, our shadow, in others. This is responsible for much acrimony in personal relationships. On a collective level it gives rise to political polarization, wars and the ubiquitous practice of scapegoating.

Again, the realization of the shadow is inhibited by the persona, the ideal image we have of ourselves. The latter is heavily influenced both by what is acceptable to others and, in a culture based on predominantly Judeo-Christian values, by the Ten Commandments. To the degree that we identify with a bright persona, our shadow is correspondingly dark. The persona aims at perfection. The shadow reminds us we are human.

We do many things under the influence of a shadow fed up with the persona. We cheat on our tax returns, lie, steal, kill and sleep with our neighbor's wife. When called to account, we wonder who did it.

The first time I stole, at age four, was from my mother's purse. "You can have a couple of pennies," she said. I took three. "Three is not a couple," my mother said with some heat. The next time was in grade two, when I snuck some candies off the teacher's desk. This was discovered and I was sternly admonished in front of the whole class. I think nothing can equal the humiliation you feel when you get a tongue-lashing in front of your friends in grade two—with your Mom watching.

But I was incorrigible. As a trusted teenage employee in a local drugstore, I regularly pocketed Hershey bars, Chiclets and peanut brittle. I knew it was wrong, but I couldn't help it. I told myself I did it because I wasn't being paid enough—that was my shadow talking. As a struggling writer my shadow lost his sweet tooth and became more practical; he only stole typewriter ribbons.

In Zurich I took to wandering around liquor stores, palming price stickers off cheap bottles and tacking them on to expensive wine.

"You're playing a dangerous game," my analyst warned. "The Swiss police have given people twenty-four hours' notice to leave the country for less serious offenses."

"My shadow did it," I insisted.

But I stopped, knowing that responsibility for what the shadow does rests squarely on the ego. That is why the existence of the shadow, once acknowledged, is a moral problem. It is one thing to realize what your shadow looks like—what you are capable of. The next step is to determine how much of it you are prepared to live out, or with. In practice, this evolves through trial and error.

Recently a top official in a major Canadian institution was fired because on his job application five years previously he had lied about his academic background. He claimed he had a graduate degree from a well-known university. A local newspaper, doing a routine story, discovered that in fact he had twice failed the final examinations. The man in question, hitherto respected and said to have had political ambitions, has just been buried by his shadow.

This is happening all the time, everywhere. In villages and cities all over the world, the unacknowledged shadow is having its say, wreaking havoc on personas and destroying lives.

There is no generally effective way to assimilate the shadow. It is more like diplomacy or statesmanship, and it is always an individual matter. Shadow and ego are like two political parties jockeying for power. If one can speak of a technique at all, it consists solely in an attitude. First one has to accept and take seriously the existence of the shadow. Second, one has to become aware of its qualities and intentions. This happens through conscientious attention to moods, fantasies and impulses. Third, a long process of negotiation is unavoidable.

However, the shadow is not only the dark underside of the conscious personality. It has a bright side too: aspects of ourselves that might yet be lived out, our unlived life—talents and abilities that have long been buried or never been conscious. They are potentially available, and their conscious realization often releases a surprising amount of energy. That is why a depressed person is counseled to go into the mood rather than try to escape it. You don't find buried treasure unless you dig.

A psychological crisis constellates both sides of the shadow: those qualities and activities we are not proud of, and new possibilities we never knew, or forgot, were there. Associated with the former is a sense of shame and moral distaste. The latter may have morally neutral connotations, but they are often more frightening because if we follow up on our dormant possibilities there is no telling what might happen.

Functionally, the shadow is complementary to the ego; one compensates the other. They can either collaborate or tear each other apart. This is a powerful and widespread archetypal motif. You find it in the Biblical stories of Cain and Abel, Isaac and Ishmael, Jacob and Esau; in Egyptian mythology there is Horus and Set. Christ and Satan represent the same theme. In Freudian terminology it is known as sibling rivalry. In Jungian psychology it is called the hostile brothers motif.

One of the world's oldest surviving myths, the Gilgamesh Epic, contains this motif as well as being instructive on other levels. Although the story doesn't end so well, it illustrates the initial conflict between an inflated ego and the instinctual shadow, a conflict one must come to grips with in order to have a balanced personality.

Gilgamesh was a young Sumerian ruler, half man and half god, who after many heroic exploits became too big for his boots. He was proud and arrogant and tyrannized his subjects. The gods sent down a brother, Enkidu, to teach him a lesson. Enkidu was an animal-man. His whole body was covered with hair. At first he roamed wild on the plains, living close to nature. He was all animal until a woman dragged him into the bush and tore off his pelt; then he became half man, familiar with lust.

Enkidu and Gilgamesh tangled at the temple gates. It was a long and nasty battle. They fought tooth and nail, but it was a stand-off in the end. They finally embraced and became best friends. Together they were half man, a quarter god and a quarter animal. For years thereafter Gilgamesh and Enkidu traveled the world defeating awesome monsters like Humbaba, guardian of the cedar forest, and the bull of heaven, a fearsome beast created by the gods, at Ishtar's request, to destroy Gilgamesh because he refused to service her.

Then Enkidu became sick and died. That was the decree of the gods, to placate Ishtar. That's the thing about gods—like autonomous complexes, what they give one day they can take away the next.

Gilgamesh was bereft. He had lost his shadow. His quest thereafter was for the elixir of life. Finally he found it in the shape of a thorny plant at the bottom of the sea. Joyfully he set off for home. But one day, as he was taking a cold bath, a snake ate the plant. Thus snakes gained the power to shed their old skin and thereby renew their life. Poor Gilgamesh gnashed his teeth and wept bitterly. He had it and he lost it!

All that, and more, was chiseled in stone. Seven thousand years ago.

The most recent manifestation of my own shadow is best described in terms of the "Riddle of the Cretan Liar," and is why I now seldom give lectures. It used to be fun, saying my piece in front of a crowd. I was an authority; people looked to me for answers and I gave them unequivocally. But one day I realized that whatever I said was problematic—the opposite was just as likely to be true, or at least worth considering.

The ancient Greeks found a convenient scapegoat for their ambivalence in the people of Crete, whom they suspected were liars—only you could never be sure because they talked in riddles.

"I am a liar," admitted one Cretan, "therefore nothing I say is true."

Well, if that was so, then this statement too was a lie, which meant everything he said *was* true. Or did it mean he only told the truth when he lied? Perhaps he was lying only when he told the truth. What's the difference anyway? And who's to say?

This shadow is tiresome, but I have learned to live with him. We tangled at the temple gates—well, my inner fences—and reached a workable compromise: I admit I could be wrong, and he lets me write books.

Conflict and Transformation

Any conflict situation constellates the problem of opposites. Broadly speaking, "the opposites" refers to the ego and the unconscious. This is true whether the conflict is recognized as an internal one or not, since conflicts with other people are almost always externalizations of an unconscious conflict within oneself. Because they are not made conscious, they are acted out on others. This is called projection, discussed in the next chapter. Here let us look more closely at the psychology of conflict.

Whatever attitude exists in consciousness, the opposite is in the unconscious. There is no way to haul this out by force. If we try, it will just refuse to come. That is why the process of analysis is unproductive unless there is an active conflict. Indeed, as long as outer life proceeds relatively smoothly, there is no need to deal with the unconscious. But when it doesn't, there is no way to avoid it.

The classic conflict situation is one in which there is the possibility of, or temptation to, more than one course of action. Theoretically the options may be many. In practice a conflict is usually between two, each carrying its own chain of consequences. In such cases the psychological reality is that two separate personalities are involved. These may be thought of as different aspects of oneself; in other words, as personifications of complexes.

Perhaps the most painful conflicts of all are those involving duty or a choice between security and freedom. Such conflicts generate a great deal of inner tension. As long as they are not conscious, the tension manifests as physical symptoms, particularly in the stomach, the back and the neck. Conscious conflict, on the other hand, is experienced as moral or ethical tension.

For instance, I have worked analytically with married men and women who had lovers on the side and troubling physical ailments. By and large, they came to me because of job-related problems or a pervading sense of meaninglessness—not because they had a conflict. Their physical symptoms passed when their right hand (ego) openly acknowledged what their left hand (shadow) was doing. There followed moral tension and a conscious search for resolution.

Conflict is a hallmark of neurosis, but conflict is not invariably neurotic. Life naturally involves the collision between conflicting obligations and incompatible desires. Some degree of conflict is even desirable, since without it the flow of life is sluggish. Conflict only becomes neurotic when it settles in and interferes with the way one functions.

I used to have a fantasy that somewhere there was a Big Book of collective wisdom called *What To Do When.* It contained the prescribed solution to all life's problems. Whenever you found yourself in a conflict you could just look it up in the book and do what it said. Such a fantasy comes from the father complex. If there were a book like that, I wouldn't have to think for myself—I'd just do what was laid down by tradition.

Alas, serious problems have only individual solutions.

Two preliminary possibilities exist for resolving a conflict. You can tally up the pro's and con's on each side and reach a logically satisfying decision, or you can opt for what you "really want," then proceed to do what is necessary to make it possible.

Many minor conflicts are amenable to reason, and those that can be decided by reason without injurious effects can safely be left to reason. But serious conflicts do not so easily disappear; in fact they often arise precisely because of a one-sided rational attitude, and thus are more likely to be prolonged than solved by reason alone.

Where this is so, it is appropriate to ask, "But what do *I* want?"—or alternatively, "What do I *want?*" Of course, if one were sure of what one wanted, one would not have a conflict in the first place. But from a psychological point of view these are still useful questions, for the first, with the accent on "I," clarifies the individual ego position (as opposed to what others might want), and the second, stressing "want," activates the feeling function (judgment, evaluation).

A serious conflict invariably involves a disparity between thinking and feeling. If feeling is not a conscious participant in the conflict, it needs to be introduced, and the same may be said for thinking.

It does sometimes happen that the ego position coincides with, or can accept, the feeling attitude. But if these are not compatible and the ego refuses to give way, then the situation remains at an impasse. That is the clinical picture of neurotic conflict, the resolution of which requires a dialogue with one's other sides (about which more later). We can learn a good deal about ourselves through relationships with others, but the unconscious is a more objective mirror of who we really are.

Jung, commenting on the psychology of conflict, was fond of referring to the Biblical parable of Buridan's ass, the donkey who starved to death between two piles of hay because he couldn't make a choice. Jung said the important thing was not whether the bundle on the right or the one on the left was the better, or which he ought to eat first, but what he wanted in the depths of his being—which did he feel pushed toward?[36]

Jung also believed that the potential resolution of a conflict is constellated by consciously holding the tension between the opposites. When every motive has an equally strong countermotive—that is, when the conflict between consciousness and the unconscious is at its peak—there is a damming up of vital energy. But life cannot tolerate a standstill. If the ego can hold the tension, something quite unexpected emerges, an irrational "third," that effectively resolves the situation.

This is what Jung called the transcendent function, which typically manifests as a symbol. Here is how he described the process:

> [A conflict] requires a real solution and necessitates a third thing in which the opposites can unite. Here the logic of the intellect usually fails, for in a logical antithesis there is no third. The "solvent" can only be of an irrational nature. In nature the resolution of opposites is always an energic

---

[36] "The Structure of the Unconscious," *Two Essays,* CW 7, par. 487.

process: she acts *symbolically* in the truest sense of the word, doing something that expresses both sides, just as a waterfall visibly mediates between above and below.[37]

Outer circumstances may remain the same, but a change takes place in
the individual. This change appears as a new attitude toward both oneself
and others; energy previously locked up in a state of indecision is re-
leased and it once again becomes possible to move forward.

At that point, it is as if you were to stand on a mountain top watching
a raging storm below—the storm may go on, but you are outside of it, to
some extent objective, no longer emotionally stressed. There is a sense of
peace. This is not essentially different from the traditional Christian concept of grace—"the peace that passeth understanding"—except that it
doesn't come from a distant God; it wells up inside.

This process requires patience and a strong ego, otherwise a decision
will be made out of desperation, just to escape the tension. But when a
decision is made prematurely—when the tension has not been held long
enough—then the other side, the option that was not chosen, will be constellated even more strongly and you're right back in the fire.

To the objection that many conflicts are intrinsically insoluble, Jung
replied that people sometimes take this view because they think only of
external solutions, which often as not are simply evasions or rationaliza-
tions of the underlying problem.

> If a man cannot get on with his wife, he naturally thinks the conflict would
> be solved if he married someone else. When such marriages are examined
> they are seen to be no solution whatever. The old Adam enters upon the
> new marriage and bungles it just as badly as he did the earlier one. A real
> solution comes only from within, and then only because the patient has
> been brought to a different attitude.[38]

In alchemical writings there is a famous precept known as the Axiom
of Maria. It goes like this: *"One becomes two, two becomes three, and
out of the third comes the one as the fourth."*[39] Jung saw this dictum as

---

[37] "The Conjunction," *Mysterium Coniunctionis,* CW 14, par. 705.
[38] "Some Crucial Points in Psychoanalysis," *Freud and Psychoanalysis,* CW 4, par. 606.
[39] *Psychology and Alchemy,* CW 12, par. 26

an apt metaphor for the process of individuation, a progressive advance of consciousness in which conflict plays a profoundly important part.

In brief, *one* stands for the original, paradisiacal state of unconscious wholeness (e.g., childhood); *two* signifies the conflict between opposites (e.g., persona and shadow); *three* points to a potential resolution; *the third* is the transcendent function; and *the one as the fourth* is alchemical code for the Philosophers' Stone—psychologically equivalent to a transformed state of conscious wholeness.

Thus simply put, individuation is a kind of circular odyssey, a spiral journey, where the aim is to get back to where you started, but knowing where you've been and what for.

The tension involved in the conflict between ego and shadow is commonly experienced as a kind of crucifixion. Surely it is no accident that the image of a man nailed to a cross has been a supreme symbol in Western civilization for two thousand years. Crucifixion symbolizes the suffering involved in growing up, the difficult process of differentiating opposites and learning to live with them. Franz Kafka pictured this literally, as a man tied to poles that could tear him apart:[40]

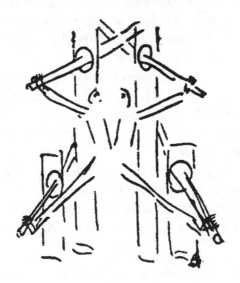

---

[40] *Letters to Milena,* p. 204.

Writes Jung:

Nobody who finds himself on the road to wholeness can escape that characteristic suspension which is the meaning of crucifixion. For he will infallibly run into things that thwart and "cross" him: first, the thing he has no wish to be (the shadow); second, the thing he is not (the "other," the individual reality of the "You"); and third, his psychic non-ego (the collective unconscious).[41]

Conflict heralds the birth of consciousness. The blissful state of unconscious wholeness, an innocent paradise symbolized in mythologies the world over as an original Edenic state, is forever sundered by the awareness of opposites. "One becomes two . . ."

Just as the Crucifixion was the culmination of Christ's earthly life, so in our daily lives its psychological equivalent, conflict, is the beginning of individuation. The Resurrection, then, is psychologically analogous to rebirth, personal transformation: what one was has died; long live the new you—if you can stand the tension.

The Puer/Puella Syndrome

The expression *puer aeternus* literally means "eternal boy." In Greek mythology it designates a child-god who is forever young, like Iacchus, Dionysus, Eros. The theme is immortalized in the modern classics *Peter Pan* and *The Picture of Dorian Gray*.

In Jungian psychology, the term "puer" is used to describe an adult man whose emotional life has remained at an adolescent level, usually coupled with too great a dependence on the mother. The term "puella" is used for a woman, though one also speaks of a woman with a puer animus—a father's daughter.[42] The puer/puella syndrome is seldom a major issue in one's early years, but many psychological crises in later life arise from the inner need to grow out of this stage.

The typical puer does not look his age and is quite proud of it. Who would not be, in a culture where youth is valued more than old age? Any

---

[41] "The Psychology of the Transference," *Practice of Psychotherapy,* CW 16, par. 470.
[42] See Marion Woodman, *The Pregnant Virgin: A Process of Psychological Transformation,* esp. pp. 35ff.

man would be shocked at the suggestion that his youthful appearance derives from emotional immaturity; ditto women.

Here is how a novelist describes her experience of puers:

> Fay knew about men who wouldn't grow up, and she wished she could tell Lizzie [her daughter], warn her. But she knew Lizzie wouldn't listen any more than she had listened.
>
> A man like this is so wildly attractive, so maddeningly alive, that he is absolutely irresistible. In the Tarot deck, he is the Fool . . . .
>
> In the picture on the card, the Fool, like a hobo, carries a sack tied to a stick. They leave you, these men, but they never said they were staying, never said they were committed, or purposeful—or responsible, even. All they want is to have a good time. And what's wrong with that? Nothing, except you begin to wonder how interested *you* are in just having a good time. . . .
>
> The joy of being with these men is the giddy return, through them, to a child's world, where there are no clocks and no claims on your time, no clothes to be kept clean, and no consequences to be considered. Days and nights are filled with the silliness, the spontaneity, the conspiratorial privacy, and all the breathless secret pleasures of life in a tree house. . . .
>
> They don't always come home, and they won't even apologize for it. They won't help around the house because they like it all messed up. They won't work very hard because they don't want to get trapped by success. And they won't work at the relationship because it's not supposed to be work, it's supposed to be fun. If you don't want to play with them, they don't mind. But that isn't going to stop them from playing.
>
> Somehow, they make you feel very old, these men. They turn you into their mother.[43]

Of course, not every woman finds such men "wildly attractive," much less irresistible. Why not? Well, following the natural "law" that we see in others traits of our own of which we are unconscious (a special case of projection), women who fall for puers are themselves quite likely to be puellas. And, as it happens, vice versa.

The typical puer shirks responsibility for his actions, and understandably so, since what he does is not within his conscious control. He is at the mercy of his unconscious, and is especially vulnerable to his instinc-

---

[43] Marsha Norman, *The Fortune Teller*, pp. 116f.

tive drives. He is prone to do what "feels right." However, he is so alienated from his true feelings that what feels right one minute often feels
wrong the next. Hence, for instance, he may find himself in erotic situations that cause him a good deal of distress the next day—or indeed that
night, in his dreams.

The individuating puer—one coming to grips with his attitudes and
behavior patterns—knows that undifferentiated feelings are highly sus-
pect, especially when they arise in conjunction with the use of alcohol or
other drugs. Instead of identifying with his feelings, he tries to keep some
distance from them, which means objectifying what he is experiencing.
He questions himself: Is this what I really feel? Is this what I want? What
are the consequences? Can I live with them? Can I live with myself?
How does what I do affect others?

Puers generally have a hard time with commitment. They like to keep
their options open, can't bear to be tied down. They act spontaneously,
with little thought of consequences. The individuating puer has to sacrifice this rather charming trait—but what he sacrifices then becomes part
of his shadow. In order then not to become an automaton, completely
ruled by habit and routine, he will have to reassimilate—this time consciously—his lapsed puer characteristics.

Also symptomatic of puer psychology is the feeling of being special,
of having a unique destiny. When you feel like that, it's hard to muster
the energy to earn a living. Compared to what you're cut out for, the
daily grind is just too mundane. This is a variety of inflation. You feel
special, so why, you ask yourself, am I doing something so ordinary?

If this attitude persists, you can cheerfully rationalize wasting your
life, waiting for destiny to catch up—or fall from the sky. You play the
lotteries and buy stocks. You know the odds are against you but you
cross your fingers and hope you'll win, and you hedge your bets with
options and silver futures.

My favorite aunt was a puella. As a grown woman she sat by the window for hours, gazing at the horizon. "One day," she would sigh, "my
ship will come in." She lived in a town on the prairies, a thousand miles
from any sea. Her husband, a frail reed of a man, worked his whole life

on an assembly line in a brewery, filling one bottle after another, drinking spillovers, dreaming of being the brewmaster.

Puers and puellas live a provisional life. There is always the fear of being caught in a situation from which it might not be possible to escape. Their lot is seldom what they really want; they are always "about to" do something, to make a change; one day they will do what is necessary—but not just yet. They speak in terms of "maybe": "Maybe I'll do this . . . maybe I'll do that . . ." Plans for the future come to nothing; life slips away in fantasies of what will be, what could be, while no decisive action is taken to change the here and now.

The provisional life is a kind of prison. The bars are the parental complexes, unconscious ties to early life, the boundless irresponsibility of the child. Thus the dreams of puers and puellas are full of prison imagery: chains, bars, cages, entrapment, bondage. Life itself, reality as they find it, is experienced as imprisonment. They yearn for independence and long for freedom, but they are powerless to pull it off.

Puers chafe at boundaries and limits and tend to view any restriction as intolerable. They do not realize that some restrictions are indispensable for growth. This is expressed in the I Ching, the Chinese book of wisdom, as follows:

> Unlimited possibilities are not suited to man; if they existed, his life would only dissolve in the boundless. To become strong, a man's life needs the limitations ordained by duty and voluntarily accepted. The individual attains significance as a free spirit only by surrounding himself with these limitations and by determining for himself what his duty is.[44]

Indeed, it is a lucky puer or puella whose unconscious eventually rebels and makes its dissatisfaction apparent through a psychological crisis. Otherwise you stay stuck and shallow.

The puer's opposite number, or shadow, is the *senex* (Latin, "old man"): disciplined, conscientious, ordered. Similarly, the shadow of the senex is the puer: unbounded instinct, disordered, intoxicated, whimsical. The puer's mythological counterpart is the Greek god Dionysus, whose frenzied female followers—puella acolytes, so to speak—ripped men to

---

[44] Hexagram 60, "Limitation," in *The I Ching or Book of Changes.*

pieces. Senex psychology is appropriately characterized by Saturn and the god Apollo: staid, rational, responsible.

It is said that the passage of time turns liberals into conservatives. Likewise, puers and puellas become old men and women, and, if they have learned from their experience, possibly even wise. But at any stage of life one must make a place for both puer and senex. In fact, whoever lives one pattern exclusively risks constellating the opposite. Enantio-dromia is waiting in the wings: the more one-sided we are, the more likely it is that the opposite will break through to spin our lives around.

I think of Norman, a former analysand. In 1970, at the age of thirty-four, he changed overnight from a dedicated family man into a fancy-free hippy—puer by another name. Hooked by the spirit of the time, he took a train across the country to San Francisco where he partied for a month. Fineglow was the name he gave his home-grown grass. He toked it all the way, stoned the whole time, and everyone he met was too. He blew his mind on Janis Joplin and Joe Cocker and Bob Dylan. He ate magic mushrooms. He mingled with beautiful people and felt great just being alive. He floated from place to place, moment to moment. He felt like a god and behaved like one. Time was electric, and so was he.

Having so much fun sapped Norman's energy. He became indolent and aimless. He felt there was nothing he couldn't do, but he didn't actually do anything. He felt creative, but he didn't create. He felt beautiful, but he did ugly things. He felt invulnerable, but he hurt a lot.

Reality and common sense, and an inner process he had no inkling of at the time, conspired to burst his bubble. Coming down was hard, but what he learned about himself in analysis was pure gold.[45] I should know, for I was that Norman.

A healthy, well-balanced personality is capable of functioning according to what is appropriate at the time. That is the ideal, seldom attained without conscious effort and a psychological crisis. Hence analysis quite as often involves the need for a well-controlled person to reconnect with the spontaneous, instinctual life as it does the puer's need to grow up.

---

[45] See my book, *The Survival Papers: Anatomy of a Midlife Crisis.*

3
The Unknown Other

*Where love reigns, there is no will to power, and where
the will to power is paramount, love is lacking.*
—C.G. Jung.

Projection and Identification

We are naturally inclined to believe that the world is as we see it, that
people are who we imagine them to be. However, we soon learn that this
is not so, because other people frequently turn out to be completely different from the way we thought they were. If they are not particularly
close, we think no more about it. If this experience involves one of our
intimates, we are devastated.

Jung was among the first to point out that we are constantly projecting
the contents of our unconscious into our environment; which is to say,
we see unacknowledged aspects of ourselves in other people. In this way
we create a series of imaginary relationships that often have little or
nothing to do with the persons we relate to.

No one can escape this. It is quite normal for unconscious contents to
be projected. That is life. Projection has generally had a bad press, but in
its positive sense it creates an agreeable bridge between people, facilitat-
ing friendship and communication. Like the persona, projection greases
the wheels of social intercourse. And as with complexes, life would be a
whole lot duller without projection.

You can also project onto things. This used to be known as having a
fetish and was generally considered to be unhealthy. People laughed at
you if you had a fascination for, say, shoes or buttons or hats or, well,
elephants. They still do, of course, but nowadays some of us know that
such things have a symbolic, psychological meaning.

There is passive projection and there is active projection. Passive projection is completely automatic and unintentional. Our eyes catch another's across a crowded room and we are smitten, head over heels. We may

know nothing about that person; in fact the less we know, the easier it is to project. We fill the void with ourselves.

Active projection is also called empathy. You feel yourself into the other's shoes by imagining what he or she is going through. This is an essential ability for an analyst. Without it there is a long succession of boring days with uninteresting people who have unimaginable problems. With it, you're on the edge.

There is a thin line between empathy and identification. Identification presupposes no separation between subject and object, no difference between me and the other person. We are two peas in a pod. What is good for me must be good for him—or her. Many relationships run aground on this mistaken notion. It is the motivation for much well-meaning advice to others, and the premise of any therapeutic system relying on suggestion or adaptation to collectively sanctioned behavior and ideals.

Therapy conducted on this basis can do more harm than good. That is why Jung insisted that those in training to become analysts must have a thorough personal analysis before being let loose. Only through an intimate knowledge of my own complexes and predispositions can I know where I end and the other begins. And even then I can't always be sure. When someone whose psychology is similar to mine shows up, I really have to be careful.

In relationships, identification is as common as potatoes and always spells trouble. Jung describes what can happen:

> When a person complains that he is always on bad terms with his wife or the people he loves, and that there are terrible scenes or resistances between them, you will see when you analyze this person that he has an attack of hatred. He has been living in *participation mystique* with those he loves. He has spread himself over other people until he has become identical with them, which is a violation of the principle of individuality. Then they have resistances naturally, in order to keep themselves apart.
>
> I say, "Of course it is most regrettable that you always get into trouble, but don't you see what you are doing? You love somebody, you identify with them, and of course you prevail against the objects of your love and repress them by your very self-evident identity. You handle them as if they were yourself, and naturally there will be resistances. It is a violation of the individuality of those people, and it is a sin against your own indi-

viduality. Those resistances are a most useful and important instinct: you have resistances, scenes, and disappointments so that you may become finally conscious of yourself, and then hatred is no more."[46]

When you identify with another person, your emotional well-being is intimately linked with the mood of that person and his or her attitude toward you. The psychology of such a situation is succinctly expressed in that old popular song, "I Want To Be Happy, But I Can't Be Happy, Till I Make You Happy Too."

It's a classic double-bind. You can't function independently and your dependence has the effect of making the other person responsible for how *you* feel. More: you have a relationship that is psychologically no different from that between parent and child. Worse: at any given moment it is hard to tell which partner is parent and which is child.

We may gladly accept this responsibility toward our children, but between grownups, in the long run, it is unworkable. Neither can make a move without double-thinking the effect on the other, which automatically inhibits the self-expression of both.

Projection, if it doesn't go as far as identification, is actually quite useful. When we assume that some quality or characteristic is present in another, and then, through experience, find that this is not true, we are obliged to realize that the world is not our own creation. If we are reflective, we can learn something about ourselves. This is called withdrawing projections. It isn't easy, it doesn't happen overnight and it's usually quite painful.

It only becomes necessary to withdraw projections when our expectations of others are frustrated. If there is no obvious disparity between what we expect, or imagine to be true, and the reality we are faced with, there is no need to withdraw projections. Don't look a gift horse in the mouth; let sleeping dogs lie—as long as they do.

Also on the positive side, it must be said that projection can constellate unrealized or dormant qualities in another person. Parental expectations notoriously lead one astray, but they can also be the stimulus to ex-

---

[46] *The Psychology of Kundalini Yoga: Notes of the Seminar Given in 1932 by C.G. Jung,* p. 7.

plore one's potential. Many a grown woman has achieved more than she might have without a friend's or lover's injunction: "You can do it!" And many a man owes his accomplishments to similar urgings. As long as power over the other, or one's own unlived life, is not lurking in the shadows, such projections do no harm at all.

Anima and Animus

The Anima

Psychologically the anima functions in a man as his soul. Jung described the anima as "the archetype of life itself."[47] When a man is full of life he is "animated." The man with no connection to his soul feels dull and listless. Nowadays we call this depression, but the experience is not new. For thousands of years, among so-called primitive peoples, this state of being has been known as loss of soul.

A man's inner image of woman is initially determined by his experience of his personal mother or closest female caregiver. It is later modified through contact with other women—friends, relatives, teachers—but the experience of the personal mother is so powerful and long-lasting that a man is naturally attracted to those women who are much like her— or, as often happens, her direct opposite. That is to say, he may yearn for what he's known, or seek to escape it at all costs.

A man who is unconscious of his feminine side is apt to see that aspect of himself, whatever its characteristics may be, in an actual woman. This happens via projection and is commonly experienced as falling in love, or, conversely, as intense dislike. A man may also project his anima onto another man, in love or hate, though in practice this is often difficult to distinguish from the projection of the man's shadow.

The man unrelated to his inner woman also tends to be moody, sometimes gentle and sentimental but prone to sudden rage and violence. Analysts call this being anima-possessed. By paying attention to his moods and emotional reactions—objectifying and personifying them—a man can come into possession of his soul rather than be possessed by it.

---

[47] "Archetypes of the Collective Unconscious," *The Archetypes and the Collective Unconscious,* CW 9I, par. 66.

As with any complex, the negative influence of the anima is reduced by establishing a conscious relationship with it.

Jung distinguished four broad stages of the anima in the course of a man's psychological development. He personified these, according to classical stages of eroticism, as Eve, Helen, Mary and Sophia.[48]

In the first stage, Eve, the man's anima is completely tied up with the mother—not necessarily his personal mother, but the image of woman as faithful provider of nourishment, security and love. The man with an anima of this type cannot function well without a vital connection to a woman and is easy prey to being controlled by her. He frequently suffers impotence or has no sexual desire at all.

In the second stage, personified in the historical figure of Helen of Troy, the anima is a collective sexual image. She is Marlene Dietrich, Marilyn Monroe, Tina Turner, Madonna, all rolled up into one. The man under her spell is often a Don Juan who engages in repeated sexual adventures. These will invariably be short-lived, for two reasons: 1) he has a fickle heart—his feelings are whimsical and often gone in the morning—and 2) no real woman can live up to the expectations that go with this unconscious, ideal image.

The third stage of the anima is Mary. It manifests in religious feelings and a capacity for genuine friendship with women. The man with an anima of this kind is able to see a woman as she is, independent of his own needs. His sexuality is integrated into his life, not an autonomous function that drives him. He can differentiate between love and lust. He is capable of lasting relationships because he can tell the difference between the object of his desire and his inner image of woman.

In the fourth stage, as Sophia (called Wisdom in the Bible), a man's anima functions as a guide to the inner life, mediating to consciousness the contents of the unconscious. Sophia is behind the need to grapple with the grand philosophical issues, the search for meaning. She is Beatrice in Dante's *Inferno,* and the creative muse in any artist's life. She is a natural mate for the archetypal "wise old man" in the male psyche. The

---

[48] "The Psychology of the Transference," *The Practice of Psychotherapy,* CW 16, par. 361; see also Marie-Louise von Franz, "The Process of Individuation," in *Man and His Symbols,* pp. 185-186.

sexuality of a man at this stage incorporates a spiritual dimension.

Theoretically, a man's anima development proceeds through these stages as he grows older. When the possibilities of one have been exhausted—which is to say, when adaptation to oneself and outer circumstances requires it—the psyche stimulates the move to the next stage.

In fact, the transition from one stage to another seldom happens without a struggle, for the psyche not only promotes and supports growth, it is also, paradoxically, conservative and loath to give up what it knows. Hence a psychological crisis is commonly precipitated when there is a pressing need for a man to move from one stage to the next.

For that matter, a man may have periodic contact with any number of anima images, at any time of life, depending on what is required to compensate the current dominant conscious attitude. The reality is that psychologically men live in a harem. Any man may observe this for himself by paying close attention to his dreams and fantasies. His soul-image appears in many different forms, as myriad as the expressions of an actual woman's femininity.

In subhuman guise, the anima may manifest as snake, toad, cat or bird; on a slightly higher level, as nixie, pixie, mermaid. In human form—to mention only a few personifications modeled on goddesses in Greek mythology—the anima may appear as Hera, consort and queen; Demeter/Persephone, the mother-daughter team; Aphrodite, the lover; Pallas Athene, carrier of culture and protectress of heroes; Artemis, the standoffish huntress; and Hecate, ruler in the netherworld of magic.

The assimilation of a particular anima-image results in its death, so to speak. That is to say, as one personification of the anima is consciously understood, it is supplanted by another. Anima development in a man is thus a continuous process of death and rebirth. An overview of this process is very important in surviving the transition stage between one anima-image and the next. Just as no real woman relishes being discarded for another, so no anima-figure willingly takes second place to her upstart rival. In this regard, as in so much else involved in a person's psychological development, the good is the enemy of the better. To have contact with your inner woman at all is a blessing; to be tied to one that holds you back can be fatal.

While the old soul-mate clamors for the attention that now, in order for the man to move on, is demanded by and due to the new one, the man is often assailed by conflicting desires. The struggle is not just an inner, metaphorical one; it also involves his lived relationships with real women. The resultant suffering and inner turmoil, the tension and sleepless nights, are comparable to what occurs in any conflict situation, as described earlier.

The dominant anima-image that must be supplanted is often characterized in fairy tales as the false bride, while the new one is called the true bride. The essential difference between the two is captured in Marie-Louise von Franz's observation: "The truth of yesterday must be set aside for what is *now* the truth of one's psychic life."[49]

True and false brides don't come labeled. A lot depends on a man's age, his position in life and how much work he's done on himself—particularly the extent to which he has already differentiated his soul-image from the other complexes teeming in his psyche.

Theoretically, there are two basic types of false bride. One is an anima figure—or an actual woman—who leads a man into the fantasy realm, away from timely responsibilities in the outside world. The other is an inner voice—or again a real woman—that would tie a man to his persona when his real task is to turn inward, to find out what's behind the face he shows others.

The first type is commonly associated with the idealistic attitudes of a younger man: the disinclination to compromise, a rigid response to the reality of everyday life. The second type of false bride is associated with regressive tendencies in later life, evident in those who make feverish efforts to mask their age or reclaim their lost youth through younger companions, fitness regimes, face lifts, hair transplants and so on.

There is no hard and fast rule, however. An older man with too much unlived life may have to descend into the whore's cellar, so to speak, as part of his individuation process. The younger man with no ideals may be forced to develop some. Such things are the daily bread of analysis.

As happens with any psychological content, the bride of either type,

---

[49] *Redemption Motifs in Fairytales*, p. 85.

when not recognized as an inner reality, appears in the outside world through projection. If a man's anima is lonely and desperate for attention, he will tend to fall in love with dependent women who demand all his time and energy. The man with a mother-bound anima will get tied up with women who want to take care of him. The man not living up to his potential will fall for women who goad him on. In short, whatever qualities a man doesn't recognize in himself—shadow, anima, whatever—will confront him in real life. Outer reflects inner, that's the general rule. If there are any psychological rules that are valid always and everywhere, that is one of them.

The seductive lure of the false bride manifests in outer life not only as a tie to an unsuitable woman but also as the wrong choice in a conflict situation. This is due to the regressive tendencies of the unconscious. Each new stage of development, each foothold on an increase in consciousness, must be wrested anew from the dragon-like grip of the past. This kind of work on oneself is called by Jung *contra naturam,* against nature. That is because nature is essentially conservative and unconscious. There is a lot to be said for the natural mind and the healthy instincts that go with it, but not much in terms of consciousness.

As the mediating function between the ego and the unconscious, the anima is complementary to the persona and stands in a compensatory relationship to it. That is to say, all those qualities absent from the outer attitude will be found in the inner. Jung gives the example of a tyrant tormented by bad dreams and gloomy forebodings:

> Outwardly ruthless, harsh, and unapproachable, he jumps inwardly at every shadow, is at the mercy of every mood, as though he were the feeblest and most impressionable of men. Thus his anima contains all those fallible human qualities his persona lacks.[50]

Similarly, when a man identifies with his persona, he is in effect possessed by the anima, with all the attendant symptoms.

> Identity . . . with the persona automatically leads to an unconscious identity with the anima because, when the ego is not differentiated from the

---

[50] "Definitions," *Psychological Types,* CW 6, par. 804.

persona, it can have no conscious relation to the unconscious processes. Consequently it *is* these processes, it is identical with them. Anyone who is himself his outward role will infallibly succumb to the inner processes; he will either frustrate his outward role by absolute inner necessity or else reduce it to absurdity, by a process of *enantiodromia*. He can no longer keep to his individual way, and his life runs into one deadlock after another. Moreover, the anima is inevitably projected upon a real object, with which he gets into a relation of almost total dependence.[51]

Thus it is essential for a man to distinguish between who he is and who he appears to be. Symptomatically, in fact, there is no significant difference between persona identification and anima possession; both are indications of unconsciousness.

The Animus

A woman's inner image of men is strongly colored by her experience of the personal father. Just as a man is apt to marry his mother, so to speak, so a woman is inclined to favor a man psychologically like her father; or, again, his opposite.

Whereas the anima in a man functions as his soul, a woman's animus is more like an unconscious mind. It manifests negatively in fixed ideas, unconscious assumptions and conventional opinions that may be generally right but just beside the point in a particular situation. A woman unconscious of her masculine side tends to be highly opinionated—animus-possessed. This kind of woman proverbially wears the pants; she rules the roost—or tries to. The men attracted to her will be driven to distraction by her whims, coldly emasculated, while she herself wears a mask of indifference to cover her insecurity.

A woman's animus becomes a helpful psychological factor only when she can tell the difference between "him" and herself. While a man's task in assimilating the anima involves discovering his true feelings, a woman must constantly question her ideas and opinions, measuring these against what she really thinks. If she does so, in time the animus can become a valuable inner companion who endows her with qualities of enterprise, courage, objectivity and spiritual wisdom.

---

[51] Ibid., par. 807.

Jung describes four stages of animus development in a woman, similar to those of the anima in a man. He first appears in dreams and fantasy as the embodiment of physical power, for instance an athlete or muscle man, a James Bond. This corresponds to the anima as Eve. For a woman with such an animus a man is simply a stud; he exists to give her physical satisfaction, protection and healthy babies.

In the second stage, analogous to the anima as Helen, the animus possesses initiative and the capacity for planned action. He is behind a woman's desire for independence and a career of her own. However, a woman with an animus of this type still relates to a man on a collective level: he is the generic husband-father, the man around the house whose primary role is to provide shelter and support for his family—Mr. Do-All, Mr. Fix-It, with no life of his own.

In the next stage, corresponding to the anima as Mary, the animus is the Word, often personified in dreams as a professor, clergyman or some other authoritarian figure. A woman with such an animus has a great respect for traditional learning; she is capable of sustained creative work and welcomes the opportunity to exercise her mind. She is able to relate to a man on an individual level, as lover rather than husband or father, and she ponders her own elusive identity.

In the fourth stage, the animus is the incarnation of spiritual meaning—a Mahatma Gandhi, Martin Luther King or Dalai Lama. On this highest level, like the anima as Sophia, the animus mediates between a woman's conscious mind and the unconscious. In mythology he appears as Hermes, messenger of the gods, or Iris, goddess of the rainbow, connecting heaven and earth; in dreams he is a helpful guide. Sexuality for such a woman is imbued with spiritual significance.

Any of these aspects of the animus can be projected onto a man, who will be expected to live up to the projected image—or else. As mentioned earlier, the same is true of the anima. So in any relationship between a man and a woman there are at least four personalities involved, as shown in the diagram opposite.[52]

---

[52] Adapted from Jung's drawing in "The Psychology of the Transference," *The Practice of Psychotherapy,* CW 16, par. 422.

Theoretically, there is no difference between an unconscious man and a woman's animus. The implication is that an unconscious man can be coerced into being or doing whatever a woman wants. But it's just as true the other way around: unconscious women are easily seduced by a man's anima. In relationships there are no innocent victims.

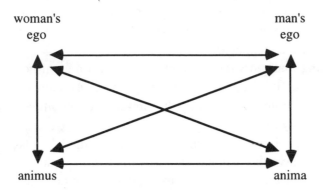

The more differentiated a woman is in her own femininity, the more able she is to reject whatever unsuitable role is projected onto her by a man. This forces the man back on himself. If he has the capacity for self-examination and insight, he may discover in himself the basis for false expectations. Failing inner resources on either side, there is only rancor and animosity.

Analogous to the true and false anima-brides discussed above, there are true and false bridegrooms. The latter may manifest as a woman's feelings of worthlessness and despair, and in her outer life as a compulsive tie to, say, an authoritarian father figure or an abusive partner. The true bridegroom gives her confidence in herself, encourages her endeavors and is interested in her mind as well as her body.

In the best of all possible worlds, the true bridegroom finds his mate in the true bride, and vice versa. Of course, this is no guarantee that they will live happily ever after. No matter how individuated one is, no matter how much one has worked on oneself, projection and conflict in relationships are always possible, if not inevitable. But that's no bad thing; we are human, after all, and such things keep us on our toes.

The Challenge of Relationship

Intimate relationships are fraught with difficulty. There are any number of landmines to be negotiated before two people feel comfortable with each other; more when they become sexually involved, and more again if and when they live together. On top of projection and identification, there are each other's personal complexes and typological differences. In truth, the very things that brought them together in the first place are just as likely to drive them apart.

Assuming that most relationships begin with mutual good will, why do so many end in acrimony? There are probably as many answers to this as there are couples who split up, but in terms of a common pattern, typology certainly plays a major role.

In general, following the logistics of Jung's model of types outlined earlier, an extraverted man has an introverted anima, while an introverted woman has an extraverted animus, and vice versa. This can change through psychological work on oneself, but these inner images are commonly projected onto persons of the opposite sex, with the result that either attitude type is prone to being fascinated by its opposite. This happens because each type is unconsciously complementary to the other.

Recall that the introvert is inclined to be reflective, to think things out and consider carefully before acting. Shyness and a degree of distrust of objects results in hesitation and some difficulty in adapting to the external world. The extravert, on the other hand, fascinated by new and unknown situations, tends to act first and think after. As Jung notes,

> The two types therefore seem created for a symbiosis. The one takes care of reflection and the other sees to the initiative and practical action. When the two types marry they may effect an ideal union.[53]

Discussing such a typical situation, Jung points out that it is ideal only so long as the partners are occupied with their adaptation to "the manifold external needs of life":

> But when . . . external necessity no longer presses, then they have time to occupy themselves with one another. Hitherto they stood back to back and

---

[53] *Two Essays,* CW 7, par. 80.

defended themselves against necessity. But now they turn face to face and look for understanding—only to discover that they have never understood one another. Each speaks a different language. Then the conflict between the two types begins. This struggle is envenomed, brutal, full of mutual depreciation, even when conducted quietly and in the greatest intimacy. For the value of the one is the negation of value for the other.[54]

Clearly such a couple has some work to do on their relationship. But that doesn't mean they ought to discuss the psychological meaning or implications of what goes on between them. Far from it. Particularly not when there is a quarrel or ill feeling in the air. It is quite enough to acknowledge that one is in a bad mood or feels hurt, as opposed to psychologizing the situation with talk of anima/animus, complexes and so on. These are after all only theoretical constructs, and head talk is sure to drive one or the other into a frenzy. Relationships thrive on feeling values, not on what is written in books.

You work on a relationship by shutting your mouth when you are ready to explode; by not inflicting your affect on the other person; by quietly leaving the battlefield and tearing your hair out; by asking yourself—not your partner—what complex in you was activated, and to what end. The proper question is not, "Why is she doing that to me?" or "Who does he think he is?" but rather, "Why am I reacting in this way?—Who do *I* think he or she is?" And more: "What does this say about my psychology? What can I do about it?" Instead of accusing the other person of driving you crazy, you say to yourself, "I feel I'm being driven crazy—where, or who, in me is that coming from?"

That is how you establish a container, a personal temenos.

It is true that a strong emotion sometimes needs to be expressed, because it comes not from a complex but from genuine feeling. There is a fine line between the two, and it is extremely difficult to tell one from the other without a container. But when you can tell the difference you can speak from the heart.

Working on a relationship involves keeping your mood to yourself and examining it. You neither bottle up the emotion nor allow it to poi-

---

[54] Ibid.

son the air. The merit in this approach is that it throws us back entirely on our experience of ourselves. It is foolish to imagine we can change the person who seems to be the cause of our heartache. But with the proper container we can change ourselves and our reactions.

It used to be thought that "letting it all hang out" was the thing to do. But that is merely allowing the complex to take over. The trick is to get some distance from the complex, objectify it, take a stand toward it. You can't do this if you identify with it, if you can't tell the difference between yourself and the emotion that grabs you by the throat when a complex is active. And you can't do it without a container.

Those who think that talking about a relationship will help it get better put the cart before the horse. Work on yourself and a good relationship will follow. You can either accept who you are and find a relationship that fits, or twist yourself out of shape and get what you deserve.

The endless blather that takes place between two complexed people solves nothing. It is a waste of time and energy and as often as not actually makes the situation worse. Jung puts it quite graphically:

> When animus and anima meet, the animus draws his sword of power and the anima ejects her poison of illusion and seduction.[55]

Of course, the meeting between anima and animus is not always negative. In the beginning, at least, the two are just as likely to be starry-eyed lovers. Later, when reality sets in and the bloom is off the rose, they may even become fast friends. But the major battles in close relationships occur because the man has not withdrawn his anima projection on the woman, and/or the woman still projects her animus onto the man.

We may understand this intellectually, but when someone we love does not behave according to the image we have of him or her, all hell breaks loose. We are instantly complexed. Our emotions do not coincide with what is in our heads. Our reactions run the gamut between outright violence, seething anger and grieved silence, depending on our psychology. Whatever the immediate reaction, it is bound to happen again unless we reflect on what is behind it.

---

[55] *Aion,* par. 30.

Intimacy with Distance

One of the greatest single obstacles to a working relationship is the ideal of togetherness. It is an ideal based on the archetypal motif of wholeness. Find your soul-mate, your other half, and you'll live happily ever after. This is a very old idea. You find it in Greek philosophy, for instance in Plato's *Symposium,* where Aristophanes pictures humans as originally whole but arrogant.[56] As punishment, Zeus cut them in half, and now we forever seek to replace our lost other.

There is nothing intrinsically wrong with this ideal. The mistake is expecting to find our "lost other" in the outside world. In fact, it is our contrasexual inner other, animus or anima, who should be the object of our search. Outer relationships, already hampered by personal complexes and a multitude of day-to-day concerns, cannot bear the extra weight of archetypal expectations. Although individuation is not possible without relationship, it is not compatible with togetherness.

Individuation, finding your own unique path, requires a focus on the inner axis, ego to unconscious—getting to know yourself. The ideal of togetherness lets you off that hook. Togetherness doesn't acknowledge the natural boundaries between people, and it gives short shrift to their differences. All you're left with is unconscious identity. When you are on the path of individuation, focused on your own psychological development, you relate to others from a position of personal integrity. This is the basis for intimacy with distance. It is not as sentimental as togetherness, but it's not as sticky either.

A relationship based on intimacy with distance does not require separate living quarters. Intimacy with distance means psychological separation, which comes about through the process of differentiation—knowing where you end and the other begins. Intimacy with distance can be as close and as warm as you want, and it's psychologically clean. Togetherness is simply fusion, the submersion of two individualities into one. That's symbiosis, identification, *participation mystique.* It can feel good for a while but in the long term it simply doesn't work.

---

[56] *Symposium,* 14-16 (189A-193E).

Togetherness is to intimacy with distance as being in love is to loving. When you're in love, you absolutely need the other. This is symptomatic of bonding, which is natural at the beginning of any relationship, at any age. But need, finally, is not compatible with loving; it only shows the degree to which one lacks personal resources. Better take your need to a therapist than dump it on the one you love. Need in an intimate relationship easily becomes the rationale for power, leading to the fear of loss on one hand, and resentment on the other.

The key to intimacy with distance is the self-containment of each of the partners, which in turn depends on how much they have worked on themselves. When you're self-contained, psychologically separate, you don't look to another person for completion. You don't identify with others and you're not victimized by their projections. You know where you stand and you live by your personal truth—come what may. You can survive cold shoulders and you can take the heat. You have what Jung calls an undivided self. Well, more or less.

When you are self-contained, you have your own sacred space, your own temenos. You might invite someone in, but you're not driven to, and you don't feel abandoned if the invitation is declined. You respect the loved one's boundaries, their freedom and privacy, even their secrets; you give them space and you don't knowingly push their buttons. You don't judge and you don't blame. There is interest in, and empathy for, the other's concerns, but you don't take them on as your own. Shoulders may be offered to cry on, but there is no plaintive plea from one to the other to be "understood."

Make no mistake: understanding what someone is saying is different from being asked to understand who is saying it. The former depends on your thinking function, and may overlap with feelings of empathy and compassion; the latter is an unconscious bid for power.

Understanding oneself is difficult enough; understanding others is their responsibility, if they are inclined to do so and have a mind for it. What one can know of another is just the tip of an iceberg; the far greater part of anyone's personal identity is beyond the ken of an outsider. For that matter, those who have worked on themselves enough to be comfortable with who they are—as opposed to those arrogant souls who are simply narcissistic—do not need, nor do they ask, to be understood by others. I am what I am; take it or leave it.

The appropriate attitude for a long-term working relationship is not understanding but *acceptance*. Each accepts the other, to the extent one can, and makes no issue of the rest. This is not easy. It means accepting not only the loved one's persona, but also his or her shadow and other complexes. It certainly requires empathy, but it also involves a mutual acknowledgment that one is responsible only for oneself.

Rilke once wrote in a letter to a friend:

> I hold this to be the highest task of a bond between two people: that each should stand guard over the solitude of the other.[57]

Personally I like the ring of that, but perhaps only an introvert could say such a thing, and maybe only another introvert—or an extravert's shadow—could appreciate it. Extraverts might rather see their "highest task" as educating a partner to the grandeur of the outer world. But typology aside, relationships suffer when you demand concurrence with your own predispositions.

When you are psychologically separate, not identified with your partner, you don't need the other to agree with you and you don't need to be right. You don't expect the other to change in order to suit your needs, and you don't ask it of yourself either. And if over time you can't accept the other but still can't leave, well, that is the stuff of analysis: conflict and complexes.

The bond between two people is a precious and mysterious thing, not entirely explained by the theory of complexes and the phenomenon of projection. But this much at least is true: there is an optimum distance in every relationship that evolves through trial and error and good will—if you know who you are and can stop pressing for more than you get.

---

[57] *Rilke on Love and Other Difficulties*, p. 28.

4
Anatomy of a Midlife Crisis

Anyone who is destined to descend into a deep pit
had better set about it with all the necessary precautions
rather than risk falling into the hole backwards.
—C.G. Jung.

Neurosis and Individuation

The juxtaposition of neurosis, usually thought of as an illness, and individuation, associated with healthy psychological development, may seem incongruous. And indeed, at first sight they are strange bedfellows.

However, in the school of thought that is called Jungian, a case may be made for neurosis as a prerequisite for the individuation process. The reason for this will become clear later. Here it is enough to note Jung's thumbnail description of neurosis as *disunity with oneself,* and individuation as *the conscious movement toward psychological wholeness.*

From this point of view, neurosis actually provides the impetus and the motivation for psychological development. In fact, if one believes in the value of becoming conscious, then those "afflicted" with neurosis are actually the lucky ones. A nervous breakdown is often a necessary prelude to a more meaningful and satisfying way of life.

A cub reporter for a local newspaper once came to interview me for a story about different approaches to therapy. "I don't know much about Jungian psychology," he said nervously. He consulted his notes. "Aren't you the people who believe in the disintegration of the personality?"

Well, I had never thought about it quite like that, but when I looked into it I found that Jung had:

A dissociation is not healed by being split off, but by more complete disintegration. All the powers that strive for unity, all healthy desire for selfhood, will resist the disintegration, and in this way he will become conscious of the possibility of an inner integration, which before he had always sought outside. He will then find his reward in an undivided self.

76

This is what happens very frequently about the midday of life, and in this wise our miraculous human nature enforces the transition that leads from the first half of life to the second.[58]

The reporter's question reminded me of a time when I refused to believe in Detroit. In my mind it stood for material values and a way of life I could not accept. And so I turned my back on Detroit and pretended it did not exist. In spite of me, however, cars continued to roll off the assembly lines and people continued to buy them.

Many things happen whether we believe in them or not. It is a fact that personalities do break down. The real question, then, is not whether but why, and to what purpose, if any.

The disintegration of the personality sounds much less ominous if it is understood as an opportunity for new life rather than the end of the line. Such an attitude is more than mere consolation for the person going through the experience; it can mean the difference between life and death, for it offers the possibility of meaning in what would otherwise be pointless suffering. This is especially true in the middle years of life, when many are brought to their knees either by circumstance or by ignorance of their own psychology, and often by both.

The factors at work in a midlife crisis are for all practical purposes indistinguishable from an acute outbreak of neurosis. Both are marked by the sudden appearance of unusual moods and behavior. The typical profile is that of a person who has always managed quite well, held down a job, perhaps married and had children, and then one day finds that nothing works any more.

Such people have dark thoughts, suspicions and fantasies that give them no peace. They lose their energy and ambition; they are anxious and feel they've missed the boat. They may ascribe their moods to the loss of a loved one, an unsatisfactory relationship, problems at work or any number of other objectively difficult circumstances. There is an inability to adapt to change; they can't meet new or unexpected situations in their usual way. Sometimes there is a strong conscious conflict—be-

[58] "Marriage as a Psychological Relationship," *The Development of Personality,* CW 17, pars. 334f.

tween loyalty to a mate, say, and attraction to an alluring other—but often there is nothing one can put a finger on. Simply said, where before they could cope with the vicissitudes of life, now they cannot. Life is a meaningless jumble. Their outlook is bleak; they hurt and have thoughts of suicide.

In Jungian analysis, relatively little attention is paid to symptoms that to others might appear to be the main problem: anxiety, conflict, depression, fear, guilt, sleeplessness, etc. and etc. Time will take care of these. The real problem lies with the psychology of the individual. Thus the aim of analysis is to bring the person's inner dynamics to light. How this is accomplished is different in every case. But the transformation of neurotic suffering into a new and healthy perspective on life—if indeed this happens—always has more to do with motivation and innate potential than with anything the analyst says or does.

The most noticeable and potentially valuable symptom in a midlife crisis is conflict. Writes Jung:

> The apparently unendurable conflict is proof of the rightness of your life. A life without inner contradiction is either only half a life or else a life in the Beyond, which is destined only for angels.[59]

The conflict between shadow and persona is invariably present in a crisis. Those who do not have such a conflict when they enter analysis soon develop one. It sometimes seems as if they had only been waiting to find someone to trust so they could safely collapse. The characteristic depression at such times indicates the need to realize that one is not all one pretends or wishes to be. The more intense the conflict, the more pressing is the need to reestablish a vital connection between consciousness and the unconscious. The struggle to bring this about is the essence of what Jung called the process of individuation.

Individuation is a process of psychological differentiation, having for its goal the development of the individual personality to its full potential. This is the goal, essentially unattainable, whose very desirability can blind one to the value and necessity of the process leading to it. As Jung

---

[59] *C.G. Jung Letters,* vol. 1, p. 375.

puts it, "The goal is important only as an idea: the essential thing is the *opus* [the work on oneself] which leads to the goal: *that* is the goal of a lifetime."[60]

In other words, the aim of the individuation process is not to overcome one's personal psychology or to become perfect, but to become familiar with it. Those who experience a psychological crisis are caught in the grip of an inner imperative to embark on the journey of self-discovery. We cannot lightly escape this obligation. Hence Jung refers to Goethe's *Faust,* where Mephisto mocks the life-weary Faust for his impulse to withdraw to the "simple life":

> Right. There is one way that needs
> No money, no physician, and no witch.
> Pack up your things and get back to the land
> And there begin to dig and ditch;
> Keep to the narrow round, confine your mind,
> And live on fodder of the simplest kind,
> A beast among the beasts; and don't forget
> To use your own dung on the crops you set![61]

Jung comments: "There is of course nothing to stop [a man] from taking a two-room cottage in the country, or from pottering about in a garden and eating raw turnips. But his soul laughs at the deception."[62]

Indeed, the simple life is an option only for those tied to it by outer necessity. The rest of us really have only two choices: to be a willing and conscious participant in our individuation or a hapless victim.

A final point: Jung believed that a good deal of personal neurosis is intimately bound up with the problems of our time, which means that it may represent an unsuccessful attempt to solve collective problems in oneself. Without being aware of it, we participate in the dominant cultural currents of the age and may reflect them in a personal conflict.

On whatever level, neurosis is best described as a symptom of self-

---

[60] "The Psychology of the Transference," *The Practice of Psychotherapy,* CW 16, par. 400.
[61] *Two Essays,* CW 7, par. 258.
[62] Ibid.

division. In many people the cause of the division is that the conscious mind wants to hold on to a moral ideal, while the unconscious strives after what seems to the ego to be immoral. People of this type always want to appear respectable, at the cost of who they really are.

But the conflict can easily be the other way around. There are those who to all appearances are wicked and unrestrained. This could be a pose, a persona, and behind their rake-hell life is a moral side which has fallen into the unconscious, just as surely as the immoral side has in the moral person. Both feel the pinch of the shadow.

The Purpose of Neurosis

The American Heritage Dictionary defines neurosis as follows:

> Any of various functional disorders of the mind or emotions, without obvious organic lesion or change, and involving anxiety, phobia, or other abnormal behavior symptoms. Also called "psycho-neurosis."

That does not sound promising, and certainly carries no hint that it might be valuable or have a purpose. It simply reflects the general view of neurosis as a sickness, as something unhealthy, abnormal. It is a natural extension of the medical, causal model of physical illness, according to which psychological symptoms have the same function as, say, a headache. They tell you the nature of an underlying problem which can then be attacked. Thus we blithely pop pills to banish depression.

Jung's view, on the other hand, is that a midlife crisis is an opportunity to become conscious—to wake up to who we are as opposed to who we think we are. Through neurosis and the symptoms that accompany it, we come face to face with our limitations—but we may also discover unknown strengths. From this standpoint neurosis is like an alarm clock, and takes on a rather more positive role than the medical community is inclined to ascribe to it.

In 1935 Jung gave a series of talks to a group of medical doctors in London. In one question period there is the following exchange:

Question: "Would Professor Jung give us a definition of neurosis?"

Jung: "A neurosis is a dissociation of personality due to the existence of complexes. To have complexes is in itself normal; but if the complexes are incompatible, that part of the personality which is too contrary to the conscious part becomes split off. . . .

"As the split-off complexes are unconscious, they find only an indirect means of expression, that is, through neurotic symptoms. . . . Any incompatibility of character can cause dissociation, and too great a split between the thinking and the feeling function, for instance, is already a slight neurosis. When you are not quite at one with yourself in a given matter, you are approaching a neurotic condition." . . .

Question: "I think we can assume, then, Professor Jung, that you regard the outbreak of a neurosis as an attempt at self-cure, as an attempt at compensation in bringing out the inferior function?"

Jung: "Absolutely."

Question: "I understand, then, that the outbreak of a neurotic illness, from the point of view of a person's development, is something favorable?"

Jung: "That is so, and I am glad you bring up that idea. That is really my point of view. . . . In many cases we have to say, 'Thank heaven he could make up his mind to be neurotic.' Neurosis is really an attempt at self-cure, just as any physical illness is partly an attempt at self-cure. . . . It is an attempt of the self-regulating psychic system to restore the balance, in no way different from the function of dreams—only rather more forceful and drastic."[63]

Jung's belief is that in a psychological crisis unconscious contents are automatically activated in an attempt to compensate a one-sided attitude of consciousness. This is true at any age, but it is not usually necessary in the first half of life to deal with what Jung calls the problem of opposites—the disparity between conscious ego attitudes and what is going on in the unconscious. The problems of young people, notes Jung,

generally come from a collision between the forces of reality and an inadequate, infantile attitude, which from the causal point of view is characterized by an abnormal dependence on the real or imaginary parents.[64]

Therapy in these cases usually involves transferring the imagos of the parents onto more suitable substitute figures, and encouraging the development of a strong ego. But for those in middle life,

---

[63] "The Tavistock Lectures," *The Symbolic Life,* CW 18, pars. 382ff.
[64] *Two Essays,* CW 7, par. 88.

development no longer proceeds via the dissolution of infantile ties, the destruction of infantile illusions and the transference of old imagos to new figures: it proceeds via the problem of opposites.[65]

Thus the ability to hold the tension in a conflict situation is of paramount importance. This is only possible when a relatively firm ego has already been established.

Jung's so-called synthetic or purposive view of neurosis is not necessarily incompatible with the traditional psychoanalytic-reductive view, namely that psychological problems are primarily sexual in nature and stem from Oedipal conflicts in childhood. It is truer to say that the two views are complementary: Freud looks to the past for the cause of psychic discomfort in the present; Jung focuses on the present with an eye to what is possible in the future.

Jung did not dispute Freudian theory that Oedipal fixations can manifest as neurosis in later life. He agreed that certain periods in life, and particularly infancy, often have a permanent and determining influence on the personality. He simply pointed out that this was an insufficient explanation for those cases in which there was no trace of neurosis until the time of the breakdown.

If the fixation were indeed real [i.e., the primary cause] we should expect to find its influence constant; in other words, a neurosis lasting throughout life. This is obviously not the case. The psycho-logical determination of a neurosis is only partly due to an early infantile predisposition; it must be due to some cause in the present as well. And if we carefully examine the kind of infantile fantasies and occurrences to which the neurotic is attached, we shall be obliged to agree that there is nothing in them that is specifically neurotic. Normal individuals have pretty much the same inner and outer experiences, and may be attached to them to an astonishing degree without developing a neurosis.[66]

What, then, determines why one person has a psychological crisis while another, perhaps in equally difficult circumstances, does not? The answer seems to be that the individual psyche knows both its limits and

---

[65] Ibid., par. 91.
[66] "Psychoanalysis and Neurosis," *Freud and Psychoanalysis*, CW 4, par. 564.

its potential. If the former are being exceeded, or the latter not realized, a breakdown occurs; the psyche itself acts to correct the situation.

The Movement of Psychic Energy

Together with the hypothesis of fixation, Freud proposed that the incestuous desires of the Oedipus complex were the primary cause of the neurotic's characteristic regression to infantile fantasies.

Although Jung accepted this view for some years, in 1913 he broke with the Vienna school of psychoanalysis when he introduced an energic viewpoint into the psychology of neurosis:

> All psychological phenomena can be considered as manifestations of energy, in the same way that all physical phenomena have been understood as energic manifestations ever since Robert Mayer discovered the law of the conservation of energy. Subjectively and psychologically, this energy is conceived as *desire*. I call it *libido*, using the word in its original sense, which is by no means only sexual.[67]

Psychic events, writes Jung, are analogous to physical events; both can be viewed from either a mechanistic or an energic stand-point:

> The mechanistic view is purely causal; it conceives an event as the effect of a cause, in the sense that unchanging substances change their relations to one another according to fixed laws. The energic point of view on the other hand is in essence final. . . . The flow of energy has a definite direction (goal) in that it follows the gradient of potential in a way that cannot be reversed.[68]

Jung felt that both views were valid, depending on the individual case. Expediency, that is to say, the possibility of obtaining results, alone decides whether the one or the other view is to be preferred.

With respect to neurosis—which both Jung and Freud saw in terms of a blockage of libido—the mechanistic or reductive view traces the problem back to a primary cause, while the energic or final view asks what is the intention of the psyche as a whole: where does the person's energy "want" to go?

---

[67] Ibid., pars. 567f.
[68] "On Psychic Energy," *The Structure and Dynamics of the Psyche,* CW 8, pars. 2f.

As indicated above, Jung suggests there is a conservation of energy within the psyche, similar to that in the physical world. He refers to the principle of equivalence, a law in physics, which states that for a given quantity of energy expended or consumed in bringing about a certain condition, an equal amount of the same or another form of energy will appear elsewhere.

Psychologically, this means that where there is an overabundance of energy in one place, some other psychic function has been deprived; conversely, when libido "disappears," as it does in a depression, it must appear in another form, for instance as a symptom.

> Every time we come across a person who has a "bee in his bonnet," or a morbid conviction, or some extreme attitude, we know that there is too much libido, and that the excess must have been taken from somewhere else where, consequently, there is too little. . . . Thus the symptoms of a neurosis must be regarded as exaggerated functions over-invested with libido.
>
> The question has to be reversed in the case of those syndromes characterized mainly by lack of libido, for instance apathetic states. Here we have to ask, where did the libido go? The libido is there, but it is not visible and is inaccessible to the patient himself. . . . It is the task of psychoanalysis to search out that hidden place where the libido dwells . . . . The hidden place is the "non-conscious," which we may also call the "unconscious" without attributing to it any mystical significance.[69]

While Jung acknowledged that reductive interpretations of neurosis can be valuable, he himself favored the energic or final viewpoint and considered it indispensable to any theory of psychological development. The causal view of regression, for instance, sees it determined by, say, a mother fixation. But from the final standpoint, writes Jung, "the libido regresses to the *imago* of the mother in order to find there the memory associations by means of which further development can take place."[70]

The difference between the personal mother and the "imago" of the mother is the difference between a complex and an archetypal image. Behind the complex—the accretion of emotional associations with one's

---

[69] "The Theory of Psychoanalysis," *Freud and Psychoanalysis,* CW 4, pars. 254f.

[70] "On Psychic Energy," *The Structure and Dynamics of the Psyche,* CW 8, par. 43.

personal mother—there is everything that has ever been associated with "mother," both positive and negative, in the history of mankind—the archetype of mother.

Regressed energy activates not only personal memories but archetypal images or symbols of, say, "mother," that may never have been personally experienced.

Jung stresses that what to the causal view is *fact,* to the final view is *symbol,* and vice versa. "Everything that is real and essential to the one is unreal and inessential to the other."[71] An exclusively causal view of neurosis may actually inhibit development, since it binds the libido to the past and to elementary facts (for instance, a fixation on the personal mother). The final view, on the other hand, encourages development by transforming causes into means to an end, "into symbolic expressions for the way that lies ahead":

> Psychic development cannot be accomplished by intention and will alone; it needs the attraction of the symbol, whose value quantum [i.e., the energy invested in it] exceeds that of the cause. But the formation of a symbol cannot take place until the mind has dwelt long enough on the elementary facts, that is to say until the inner or outer necessities of the life-process have brought about a transformation of energy.[72]

The transformation of energy in this way is central to Jung's idea of what happens in neurosis. It involves both the principle of equivalence, mentioned above, and the principle of entropy, according to which the transformation of energy in a closed system is only possible as a result of differences in the intensity of energy that exists between different elements in that system.

Mix a glass of hot water with cold, for instance, and you end up with warm water. The transfer of energy from one to the other leads to an equalization of differences. Within the system there is a transformation. Jung applied this principle to the psyche, with specific reference to what occurs in a conflict situation:

---

[71] Ibid., par. 45.
[72] Ibid., par. 47.

Psychologically, we can see this process at work in the development of a lasting and relatively unchanging attitude. After violent oscillations at the beginning the opposites equalize one another, and gradually a new attitude develops, the final stability of which is the greater in proportion to the magnitude of the initial differences. The greater the tension between the pairs of opposites, the greater will be the energy that comes from them. . . .

Daily psychological experience affords proof of this . . . . The most intense conflicts, if overcome, leave behind a sense of security and calm which is not easily disturbed, or else a brokenness that can hardly be healed. Conversely, it is just these intense conflicts and their conflagration which are needed in order to produce valuable and lasting results.[73]

Jung compared the flow of libido to a river: "The libido has, as it were, a natural penchant: it is like water, which must have a gradient if it is to flow."[74] This is an eminently practical consideration in a psychological crisis, where the flow of energy is blocked. The problem in each particular case is to find the appropriate gradient, the object or direction toward which the energy naturally "wants" to go. "What is it," asks Jung, "at this moment and in this individual, that represents the natural urge of life? That is the question."[75]

This regularly raises a moral dilemma and heightens an already existing conflict, which is precisely what is required. "There is no energy unless there is a tension of opposites," writes Jung. "Hence it is necessary to discover the opposite to the attitude of the conscious mind."[76] This involves bringing to light psychic contents that have been repressed.

The repressed content must be made conscious so as to produce a tension of opposites, without which no forward movement is possible. The conscious mind is on top, the shadow underneath, and just as high always longs for low and hot for cold, so all consciousness, perhaps without being aware of it, seeks its unconscious opposite, lacking which it is doomed to stagnation, congestion, and ossification. Life is born only of the spark of opposites.[77]

---

73 Ibid., pars. 49f.
74 *Symbols of Transformation,* CW 5, par. 337.
75 *Two Essays,* CW 7, par. 487.
76 Ibid., par. 78.
77 Ibid.

Adaptation and Breakdown

The process of development from child to adult entails an increasing adaptation to the external world. Whenever a person's libido, in the process of adaptation, meets an obstacle, there is an accumulation of energy that normally gives rise to an increased effort to overcome the obstacle.

But if the obstacle seems to be insurmountable and the individual abandons the task of overcoming it, the stored-up energy regresses, that is, reverts to an earlier mode of adaptation. This in turn, writes Jung, activates infantile fantasies and wishes:

> The best examples of such regressions are found in hysterical cases where a disappointment in love or marriage has precipitated a neurosis. There we find those well-known digestive disorders, loss of appetite, dyspeptic symptoms of all sorts, etc. . . . [typically accompanied by] a regressive revival of reminiscences from the distant past. We then find a reactivation of the parental imagos, of the Oedipus complex. Here the events of early infancy—never before important—suddenly become so. They have been regressively reactivated. Remove the obstacle from the path of life and this whole system of infantile fantasies at once breaks down and becomes as inactive and ineffective as before.[78]

For these reasons, Jung declared that he did not seek the cause of a neurosis in the past, but in the present: "I ask, what is the necessary task which the patient will not accomplish?"[79] In other words, in terms of the developmental process described above, "the psychological trouble in neurosis . . . can be formulated as *an act of adaptation that has failed.*"[80]

As already indicated, this view of neurosis is quite different from the classical Freudian view, but it does not substantially change what happens in the process of analysis. The fantasies still have to be brought to light because the energy the person needs for health—that is, for adaptation—is attached to them. The object, however, is not to reveal a supposed root cause of the neurosis but to establish a connection between the conscious mind and the unconscious. Only in this way can the split-

---

[78] "Psychoanalysis and Neurosis," *Freud and Psychoanalysis,* CW 4, par. 569.
[79] Ibid., par. 570.
[80] Ibid., par. 574.

off energy become available for the accomplishment of the "necessary task" the person balks at.

> Considered from this standpoint, psychoanalysis no longer appears as a mere reduction of the individual to his primitive sexual wishes, but, if rightly understood, as a highly moral task of immense educational value.[81]

Jung's view of neurosis as an attempt at self-cure, and his application of the conservation of energy theory to psychological phenomena, are cornerstones in the practice of analytical psychology. A working assumption in the case of depression, for instance, is that the energy not available to consciousness has not simply vanished but is busily stirring up unconscious contents that for the sake of psychological health need to be brought to light and examined. Thus, while a well-meaning friend might advise a depressed person to seek out a distraction, the analyst sees the depression, or indeed any overwhelming mood, as a challenge to find out what is going on inside. Hence one is encouraged to introspect, to stay with the mood, to go into it rather than try to escape it.

In the normal course of life there is a relatively easy progression of libido, which is to say one's energy may be directed more or less at will. Jung defines progression as "the daily advance of the process of psychological adaptation."[82] This is not the same as development; progression refers simply to the continuous flow or current of life.

In order to satisfy the demands of adaptation it is necessary to adopt or attain an attitude appropriate to given circumstances. As long as circumstances do not change, there is no reason for one's attitude to change. But since circumstances do change, whether suddenly or over time, there is no one attitude that is permanently suitable.

Any change in the environment demands a new adaptation, which in turn requires a change in the attitude that was previously quite adequate. But a suitable attitude—that is, one that works in a given situation—is invariably characterized by a certain one-sidedness and is therefore resistant to change. When a particular attitude is no longer appropriate for the external situation, the stage is set for neurosis.

---

[81] Ibid., par. 575.
[82] "On Psychic Energy," *The Structure and Dynamics of the Psyche*, CW 8, par. 60.

For example, a feeling-attitude that seeks to fulfil the demands of reality by means of empathy may easily encounter a situation that can only be solved through thinking. In this case the feeling-attitude breaks down and the progression of libido ceases. The vital feeling that was present before disappears, and in its place the psychic value of certain conscious contents increases in an unpleasant way; subjective contents and reactions press to the fore and the situation becomes full of affect and ripe for explosions.[83]

Such symptoms indicate a damming up of libido, which is always marked by the breaking up of pairs of opposites.

During the progression of libido the pairs of opposites are united in the co-ordinated flow of psychic processes. . . . But in the stoppage of libido that occurs when progression has become impossible, positive and negative can no longer unite in co-ordinated action, because both have attained an equal value which keeps the scales balanced. . . . The tension leads to conflict, the conflict leads to attempts at mutual repression, and if one of the opposing forces is successfully repressed a dissociation ensues, a splitting of the personality, or disunion with oneself.[84]

The struggle between the opposites would continue unabated if the process of regression, the backward movement of libido, did not set in with the outbreak of the conflict.

Through their collision the opposites are gradually deprived of value and depotentiated. . . . In proportion to the decrease in value of the conscious opposites there is an increase in value of all those psychic processes which are not concerned with outward adaptation and therefore are seldom or never employed consciously.[85]

As the energic value of these previously unconscious psychic processes increases, they manifest indirectly as disturbances of conscious behavior and those emotional symptoms characteristic of neurosis.

Jung's view is that since the stoppage of libido is due to a failure of the dominant conscious attitude, the unconscious contents activated by regression contain the seeds of a new progression. In terms of his model

---

[83] Ibid., par. 61.
[84] Ibid.
[85] Ibid., par. 62.

of typology, the unconscious contents include one's opposite attitude which, with the inferior functions, is potentially capable of complementing or even of replacing the inadequate conscious attitude.

> If thinking fails as the adapted function, because it is dealing with a situation to which one can adapt only by feeling, then the unconscious material activated by regression will contain the missing feeling function, although still in embryonic form, archaic and undeveloped. Similarly, in the opposite type, regression would activate a thinking function that would effectively compensate the inadequate feeling.[86]

The regression of energy thus confronts us with the problem of our own psychology, as opposed to the initial difficulty of adapting to outer circumstances. In Jung's words, "regression leads to the necessity of adapting to the inner world of the psyche."[87]

The aspects of the "inner world" that we need to become aware of in such a situation are of course the complexes, and particularly our persona, anima or animus, and shadow. Looked at in this way, regression is not an abnormal symptom but as much a necessary phase in the developmental process as is progression.

It might seem from this description that the progression of energy — adaptation to outer conditions—is conceptually analogous to extraversion, and regression—requiring adaptation to inner conditions—is comparable to introversion. According to Jung, this is not the case:

> Progression is a forwards movement of life in the same sense that time moves forwards. This movement can occur in two different forms: either extraverted, when the progression is predominantly influenced by objects and environmental conditions, or introverted, when it has to adapt itself to the conditions of the ego (or, more accurately, of the "subjective factor"). Similarly, regression can proceed along two lines: either as a retreat from the outside world (introversion), or as a flight into extravagant experience of the outside world (extraversion). Failure in the first case drives a man into a state of dull brooding, and in the second case into leading the life of a wastrel.[88]

---

[86] Ibid., par. 65.
[87] Ibid., par. 66.
[88] Ibid., par. 77.

The Self-regulation of the Psyche

The Jungian view of neurosis as an attempt at self-cure is based on the belief that the psyche is a self-regulating system. In Jung's memorable statement, "Only what is really oneself has the power to heal."[89]

Indeed, if I were asked to choose one remark of Jung's that informs my attitude as an analyst, that would be it. The whole process is there. And what is really oneself can only be discovered through holding the tension between the opposites until a third—the *tertium non datur,* the third not logically given—manifests. How this "third," the so-called transcendent function, makes itself known depends on individual psychology and circumstances. But in Jung's model it always represents the creative intervention and guidance of the Self, the archetype of wholeness, which functions as the regulating center of the psyche.

In plainer words, the Self is a transpersonal power that is beyond the control of the ego. It can be experienced, but not easily defined. In fact, there is no difference between the Self as an experiential, psychological reality and the religious concept of a supreme being, except that the traditional idea of God places him somewhere "out there." In Jung's model of the psyche, the Self is inside.

Here are some significant comments by Jung on the Self:[90]

Intellectually the self is no more than a psychological concept, a construct that serves to express an unknowable essence which we cannot grasp as such, since by definition it transcends our powers of comprehension. It might equally well be called the "God within us."

The self could be characterized as a kind of compensation of the conflict between inside and outside. . . . [It] has somewhat the character of a result, of a goal attained, something that has come to pass very gradually and is experienced with much travail. So too the self is our life's goal, for it is the completest expression of that fateful combination we call individuality.

Sensing the self as something irrational, as an indefinable existent, to which the ego is neither opposed nor subjected, but merely attached, and

---

[89] *Two Essays,* CW 7, par. 258.
[90] Note: Jung did not always capitalize the term "Self," but in modern Jungian writing it is conventional to do so, in order not to confuse the Self as archetype with the ego-self.

about which it revolves very much as the earth revolves round the sun—thus we come to the goal of individuation.[91]

Like any archetype, the essential nature of the Self is unknown and possibly unknowable, but its manifestations—archetypal images of the Self—are known to us all, in one form or another, as the content of dreams, myth and legend.

> The self appears in dreams, myths, and fairytales in the figure of the "supraordinate personality," such as a king, hero, prophet, saviour, etc., or in the form of a totality symbol, such as the circle, square, *quadratura circuli,* cross, etc. When it represents a *complexio oppositorum,* a union of opposites, it can also appear as a united duality, in the form, for instance, of *tao* as the interplay of *yang* and *yin,* or of the hostile brothers, or of the hero and his adversary (arch-enemy, dragon), Faust and Mephistopheles, etc. Empirically, therefore, the self appears as a play of light and shadow, although conceived as a totality and unity in which the opposites are united.[92]

*

A summary of the typical progression of psychological events in a midlife crisis appears opposite.

---

[91] Ibid., pars. 399f.
[92] "Definitions," *Psychological Types,* CW 6, par. 790.

The Self-regulation of the Psyche

1. Difficulty of adaptation. Difficulty of progression of energy.

2. Regression of libido (depression, lack of disposable energy).

3. Activation of unconscious contents (infantile fantasies, complexes, archetypal images, inferior function, opposite attitude, shadow, anima/animus, etc.). Compensation.

4. Formation of neurotic symptoms (confusion, fear, anxiety, guilt, moods, emotional reactions, etc.).

5. Unconscious or half-conscious conflict between the ego and contents activated in the unconscious. Inner tension. Defensive reactions.

6. Activation of the transcendent function, involving the Self and archetypal patterns of wholeness.

7. Formation of symbols (numinosity, synchronicity).

8. Transfer of energy between unconscious contents and consciousness. Enlargement of the ego, more adequate progression of energy.

9. Integration of unconscious contents. Active involvement in the process of individuation.

5
The Analytic Experience

Analysis should release an experience that grips us or falls upon us from above, an experience that has substance and body such as those things which occurred to the ancients. If I were going to symbolize it I would choose the Annunciation.
—C.G. Jung.

Getting Started

You can appreciate the scope of Jung's work, and you can read everything he ever wrote, but the real opportunity offered by analytical psychology only becomes apparent when you go into analysis. That's when Jung's potentially healing message stops being merely an interesting idea and becomes an experiential reality.

Analysis is not a suitable discipline for everyone, nor does everyone benefit from it or need it. But when you are overwhelmed by conflict or difficulties in a relationship, or when you feel your life has no meaning, you could do worse than see a Jungian. Although there may be as many ways of practicing Jungian analysis as there are analysts, the process itself facilitates healing because it relates what is going on in the unconscious to what is happening in everyday life.

We generally seek a quick fix to our problems. We want an answer, a prescription; we want our pain to be treated, our suffering relieved. We want a solution, and we look for it from an outside authority. This is a legitimate expectation for many physical ills, but it doesn't work with psychological problems, where you are obliged to take personal responsibility for the way things are. Then you have to consider your shadow— and everyone else's—and all the other complexes that drive you and your loved ones up the wall.

What people want and what they need are seldom the same thing. You go into analysis hurting and with some goals and expectations in mind. But pretty soon your personal agenda goes out the window and you find yourself grappling with issues you hadn't thought of and sore spots you didn't know were there—or knew but avoided thinking about. It is very exciting, all this new information about yourself. It's inevitably inflating, and for a while you think you have all the answers—but it can also be quite painful, since things generally get worse before they get better.

It has been said that analysis is only for an elite because it's expensive and time-consuming. It is true that analysis involves a good deal of time and energy and it's not cheap. But I have worked with teachers and taxi-drivers, doctors, actors, politicians, artists—men and women in just about every walk of life. Not one of them was independently wealthy. The fee they paid was no small matter. They were able to afford it by making sacrifices in other areas of their life. It is a matter of priorities— you put your money, your energy, into what you value, and if you hurt enough you find a way.

Jungian analysis is not about improving yourself. It doesn't make you a better person, and it doesn't insulate you from the slings and arrows of everyday life. Analysis is about becoming conscious of who you are, including your strengths and weaknesses. Analysis is not something that's done to you. It is a joint effort by two people focused on trying to understand what makes you tick.

In the process of working on yourself you will change, and that can create new problems. Others may not like what you become, or you may no longer like them. Indeed, it may be that as many relationships break up through analysis as are cemented. When you become aware of your complexes, and start taking back what you have projected onto a partner, you may discover there is not much left to hold you together. A difficult experience, certainly, but the sooner you realize you aren't in the right place, the better. Analysis makes it possible to live one's experiential truth and accept the consequences.

The particular circumstances that take a person into analysis are as multitudinous as grains of sand on a beach. They are both as unique and as similar as one grain of sand is to another. True, the reasons are always related to one's personal psychology and life situation. But behind such individual details there are general patterns of thought and behavior that have been experienced and expressed since the beginning of mankind.

An understanding of these patterns, found the world over in myths, fairy tales and religions—manifestations of what Jung called the archetypes—gives one a perspective on mundane reality. A knowledge of archetypes and archetypal patterns is a kind of blueprint, or background tapestry, against which our individual complexes are played out. It is an indispensable tool for Jungian analysts, and an overtone that fundamentally distingushes Jungian analysis from any other form of therapy.

Knowledge gained from books is all well and good, but true healing does not happen in the head; it occurs through feeling-toned realizations in response to lived experience. That is why the analytic process, when pursued on an intellectual level—and that includes most self-analysis—is sterile. Jung underlines this:

> As long as an analysis moves on the mental plane nothing happens, you can discuss whatever you please, it makes no difference, but when you strike against something below the surface, then a thought comes up in the form of an experience, and stands before you like an object . . . . Whenever you experience a thing that way, you know instantly that it is a fact.[93]

Such "thoughts in the form of an experience" have a transforming effect because they are numinous, overwhelming. They lead to a more balanced perspective: one is merely human—not entirely good (positive inflation), not entirely bad (negative inflation), but a homogenous amalgam of good and evil. The realization and acceptance of this is a mark of the integrated personality.

The process of assimilating unconscious contents does not happen without work. It requires discipline and concentrated application—and a mind receptive to the numinous. Like my attention to the meaning, for me, of elephants. Here are some things I learned about them after that fateful find in the hills of Zurich:

Queen Maya, the Buddha's mother, dreamed that a white elephant entered her womb the night she conceived the savior, an event analogous to the Virgin Mary's Annunciation—and to the experience of analysis.

---

[93] Jung, *The Visions Seminars,* pp. 337f.

Astrologically, elephants, along with donkeys, lobsters and other shellfish, are ruled by Capricorn. (I am a Capricorn, January 2.)

In Kundalini yoga the elephant is the symbol for the *muladhara* chakra, the lowest spiritual center, located between the anus and the genitals. It is particularly active, they say, when one is depressed.

An elephant's height is roughly three-and-a-half times the circumference of its front foot. The longest recorded length of an elephant penis is six feet, flaccid.

It is said that an elephant's trunk in the down position means it is unhappy and might attack; in the up position, it is in a good mood. I read this as: down, time to stare at the wall; up, ready to party.

An old Hindu myth tells how elephants once could fly and change shape like clouds. One day a flock landed on the branch of a tree and killed a holy man. From that time on they were condemned to walk on land. This is comparable psychologically to those who come down to earth after flying too high (e.g., puers).

Elephant sounds include barks, snorts, trumpets, roars, growls and rumbles. Many are below our range of hearing, in what is known as infrasound, also generated by earthquakes, wind, thunder, volcanoes and ocean storms. (Which is to say, they are good complex indicators.)

An elephant's trunk is powerful yet flexible, housing a keen sense of smell. It can uproot trees, flick with deadly force, suck up and expel almost anything, or sniff and pluck flowers (like a union of the opposite functions, sensation and intuition).

Elephants have thick skins, impervious to ants, gnats and other pesky insects (e.g., complexes). The elephant's most formidable enemy is the snake, ubiquitous symbol of the unconscious. (I painted snakes too, and once I got an elephant and a snake to kiss—another union of opposites.)

Elephants do what is right in front of them. As far as we know, they do not long to be tigers; they are content to be who they are. According to some Indian myths, they are solid enough to support the world.

I read a newspaper article about a man who had brought up two elephants from infancy and then sold them. After a time he felt they weren't being well cared for, so he took them back in the middle of the night.

Police and FBI agents were alerted. Three months later he and they were still at large. His daughter said, "It is not easy hiding out with a couple of elephants six and seven feet tall. All I can say is my father is a very clever man." (Ah. Puella defending puer father who identifies with elephants? A man who knows where he stands? Interesting possibilities.)

D.H. Lawrence wrote a poem called "The Elephant Is Slow To Mate." It starts like this:

> The elephant, the huge old beast,
>   is slow to mate;
> he finds a female, they show no haste
>   they wait . . .

And imagine my delight when I, on my knees, chanced upon these words by Jung: "I have dreamt several times of elephants which I always had to treat warily. Apparently they were engaged in road-building."[94]

Now, twenty years later, elephants are not quite as numinous to me, but I still wear a tiny gold one on a chain around my neck. I would not know as much about myself as I do, and I would not have become what I am, if I had kicked that first one aside.

Jung purposely did not develop a systematic therapeutic method or technique, as did Freud for instance. But Jung did describe four characteristic stages of the analytic process: confession, elucidation, education and transformation.[95]

In the first stage, you get things off your chest. Its prototype is the confessional practice of almost all the mystery religions of antiquity and their historical continuation in the Catholic Church. You confess to the analyst everything consciously concealed, repressed, guilt-laden, etc.— thoughts, wishes, fantasies, emotions like fear, hate, aggression and so on, and whatever else you are not proud of.

In the second stage, *elucidation,* you become aware of personal unconscious contents that have not been concealed or repressed but rather

---

[94] *Letters,* vol. 2, p. 118.
[95] See "Problems of Modern Psychotherapy," *The Practice of Psychotherapy,* CW 16, pars. 122ff.; also Marie-Louise von Franz, *C.G. Jung: His Myth in Our Time,* pp. 66ff.

have never been conscious: dormant character traits, attitudes and abilities. You develop an understanding of complexes, projection, persona and shadow, anima/animus, and become aware of a regulating center, the Self. This comes about mainly through close attention to your responses to daily events and the nightly images in your dreams.

Once these contents have been assimilated to consciousness, the next task is that of *education,* which refers to discovering your role as a social being—your place in the world, where you fit in, your vocation.

In the fourth stage, *transformation,* you become more fully the person you were always meant to be. Unconscious compulsion is replaced by conscious development; aimless activity gives way to a directed focus on what is personally relevant and meaningful. Egocentricity is subsumed by a working relationship with the Self.

This process of maturation, although not the only possible sequence, is essentially what Jung meant by individuation. It takes time and effort and usually involves some sacrifice along the way, but it can happen.

Work on What Has Been Spoiled

I was in analysis for about two months before I cried in front of my analyst. Whatever happened outside, in my analytic hours I was determined to be a man. I wanted to impress my analyst; I wanted him to like and respect me. I had an urbane persona to live up to, my image of myself. I would not willingly drop it in front of him. He was the person in whose eyes I most wanted to shine, and so I never told him how I really felt about anything. I feared he would judge me as weak.

This charade came to an end the day his comments struck a nerve that was so raw my defenses failed. At the time I thought it was quite accidental. Today, having pushed a few buttons myself, I'm not so sure.

I remember it well. It was a bright and cloudless Thursday morning. That is not usual in Zurich. Even when the surrounding mountains are bathed in sunshine, the city is usually overcast and gray. Meteorologically, Zurich invites depression. The weather reports speak more often of lows than highs, and the same was true of me.

My analyst's office was lined with bookshelves. Plants and personal mementos were everywhere. I loved that place. Once a week I sat there for an hour and felt safe. Well, safer than anywhere else.

"It was a good week," I lied.

Should I tell him about my crying in the night? Should I tell him how lonely I was, how I felt about my housemate's interminable parties? Would he be interested to know that I got into bed with two women one night and couldn't get an erection? What would he think if I told him I was afraid of dogs? Of heights? How would he react to my prowling the Niederdorf, Zurich's red light district? Should I tell him about my experiments with dope? About the woman who bit me in a pub?

I forced a smile. "Nothing special."

I read from my journal, my usual routine. I had diligently recorded each day's events—edited to make me look good—followed by the dreams that night and my associations to their bizarre images. I amplified the themes from mythology and religion and reflected at length on their psychological meaning.

No doubt about it, I was a prize student. I did everything I was supposed to. I could not be faulted on procedure.

"And what else?" asked my analyst, smoothing the top of his head where no hair grew.

"What else what?" I said, looking up.

"What else occurs to you," he said. "What else about this woman in your dream, this unknown female who asks you for a dance?"

"Well, she's my anima, isn't she?"

"I don't speak Greek," said my analyst. "Explain, please."

I leaned back, confident. "The anima is my inner woman," I said. "Everybody knows that. Apparently she wants to get closer to me. Well," I laughed, "I wouldn't mind."

My analyst leaned forward. "Why are you here?" he asked.

I cringed. Tears stung my eyes. I opened my mouth to speak and nothing came out. For a few minutes I cried uncontrollably. I also had the hiccups.

I wiped my face. "Sorry about that," I said. "I don't know what came over me."

My analyst looked quite stern. His eyes were slightly in shadow from the reading lamp between us. He clasped and unclasped his hands. I felt naked, stripped to the bone. I hung there, expecting to be banished. My eyes took in his books, his antique desk, the lush green plants, an upright piano in one corner, the window looking to the lake. I fastened on his bald spot, waiting. Please God, I thought, do not tell me I'm unworthy.

Then he smiled, openly, full face, a rare occurrence that to me sang of acceptance. He rubbed his hands. "Now we do analysis," he said, "if that's what you want."

That was some twenty-five years ago. I still remember that session, and many others, because they were turning points. On that Thursday morning I developed a degree of trust for my analyst that hadn't been there before. I broke down and it was okay. After that I left my persona at the door with my umbrella.

Another landmark was the day I realized I'd been avoiding my real task by taking to the hills whenever I felt depressed.

At that time I was living in a small village outside Zurich, an area of great natural beauty. The lower Alps were my back yard. I would often set out on a hike in the early morning and not return till late afternoon. I described it to my analyst: bright sun sparkling on snowy peaks, multi-colored wildflowers, cute little animals starting in the brush, a deep refreshing silence barely disturbed by bird calls and the occasional staff-toting Teuton. Once I found a dead ringer of a Clint Eastwood hat, right out of *Fistful of Dollars*.

"It's so wonderful," I said. "All my cares disappear. I feel at one."

My analyst raised his eyebrows. I think he did that for effect; I was always a bit apprehensive when he raised his eyebrows.

"At . . . one," he said, slowly rolling the words. "What exactly does that mean?"

"Peace," I replied gamely. "Bliss . . . no conflict, no pain."

He nodded. "I see—swallowed by the great maw. You feel good just being. It relieves you of having to become conscious."

Then I got down to work, and yes, things did get worse before they got better.

When I first entered analysis it was just another course to me, like being at university. The goal, I thought, was grades. You did your best and
you passed or failed.

Wrong. In the process of analysis your best is not what you have to
offer intellectually, nor is your worst. The goal is individuation, but even
that, in Jung's words quoted earlier, is important only as an idea.[96]
Moreover, you are graded not on what is in your head, but on who you
are becoming. And even then, not by your analyst.

There are a lot of dull hours in analysis when nothing seems to be
happening. Of course there is the occasional Eureka! but change sometimes takes years. The revelations, the insights, come only after prolonged attention to the mundane. This is quite a shock to those who go
into analysis seeking the divine.

People have come to me because they wanted to understand their visions. When they realize there is nothing special about having visions,
that they're as common as turnips and that their task is to come down to
earth, they stop analysis. People come because they *want* to have visions.
I send them away. I have a profound respect for spontaneous visions.
Like dreams, they can be a valuable source of information about what is
going on in the unconscious, in terms of compensating one's conscious
attitudes. But I have no idea how to create visions, and going looking for
them makes no sense to me at all.

There are others who seek analysis because they think it will make
them gods, invulnerable. They stop because it doesn't. Some go into
analysis just because they think it's a good idea. They don't last long either; there's no edge. And there are those who stop out of sheer frustration; they can't make the connection between what goes on at night, in
their dreams, and what happens in their waking life.

Daily life is the raw material of analysis. It is analogous to what the alchemists called the *prima materia,* the lead or base metal they strived to
turn into gold by melting and running its vapors through flasks and re-
torts, a process of distillation similar to making strong liquor from wine.

---

[96] Above, p. 79.

The alchemists' *distillatio* is akin psychologically to the process of discrimination: the differentiation of our moods and dreams, attitudes, feelings and thoughts, with close attention to the nitty-gritty detail of conflict in relationships—the "he said," "she said" encounters that bring you to a boil at first, and make you cringe when you cool down.

All this, the base metal of your miserable life, you write down in a journal. That takes some discipline, but if you don't write it down you don't remember. Of course you can't record everything. You'd get lost in the forest and miss the trees. You note the highlights, particularly emotional reactions—because they signal the activation of complexes—and your conscious attitude toward them. You reflect on all this, mull it over, and then you take it to your analyst.

Time is a big factor in this process. An hour or two a week with an analyst is never enough, but when it's all you've got you soon get used to it. In any case, the real work is what you do on your own between sessions; and if you don't do much on your own, then very little happens.

The demands of working on oneself are many and varied. One day you get up at four a.m. to attend to what's bugging you. The next day you sleep till noon, flooded with dreams. At night you stare at the wall, read and make notes, take in a movie or watch television, or maybe you go to a noisy pub with friends. You try to pick and choose when to go out and when to go in—but at times you are chosen.

I think of Rilke's description of his neighbor, a Russian bureaucrat named Nikolai Kusmitch.[97] Time was precious to Nikolai Kusmitch. He spent his days hoarding it, saving a second here, a minute or two there, sometimes a whole half hour. He imagined that the time he saved could be used to better advantage when he wasn't so busy. Perhaps it could even be tacked on at the end of his life, so he'd live longer.

He sought out what he thought must certainly exist: a state institution for time, a kind of Time Bank you could make deposits in and then draw on. He didn't find one, so he kept the loose change in his head.

Nikolai Kusmitch did what he could to economize, but after a few

---

[97] *The Notebook of Malte Laurids Brigge,* pp. 161ff.

weeks it struck him that he was spending too much.

"I must retrench," he thought.

He rose earlier. He washed less thoroughly, ate his toast standing up and drank coffee on the run. But on Sundays, when he came to settle his accounts, he always found that nothing remained of his savings. Alas, he died as he had lived, a pauper.

Working on yourself is something like that. You can't save it up for Sundays; it's what you do during the week that counts.

The Wounded Healer

As noted earlier, Jung suggested that personality is made up of an ego and any number of island complexes. The task in analysis is to establish a beachhead on the ego-mainland that is a more satisfactory living space than "happy neurosis island" (as one of Jung's patients described it),[98] and at the same time make friends with the animals—the instincts—in the unconscious. That is what can happen, via projection, in analysis.

In a formal therapeutic setting, the projection of unconscious contents is known as the transference: the analysand's beachhead, the still-unconscious healing "answer," is projected onto the analyst, whose response is called countertransference. It's a set-up. The analyst knows both that he is expected to heal and that he cannot. More: he can be tricked into believing he can.

The transference is as many-headed as the mythical Hydra and has as many arms as an octopus. The analyst parries their thrusts as best he can while he waits for the healing factor to constellate in the analysand. This is in accord with the fundamental Jungian belief in the psyche as a self-regulating system. But just how healing happens, if and when it does, has given rise to speculation about a wounded healer archetype.

The term "wounded healer" derives from the work of Asclepius, a legendary Greek doctor who in recognition of his own suppurating sores set up a sanctuary where others could come to be healed of theirs.[99]

---

[98] "Psychology of the Transference," *The Practice of Psychotherapy,* CW 16, par. 374.
[99] See C.A. Meier, *Ancient Incubation and Modern Psychotherapy.*

Those seeking to be cured went through a process called incubation. First they had a cleansing bath. This was thought to have a purifying effect on the soul as well as the body. After some preliminary sacrificial offerings, the incubants lay on a couch—Greek *cline,* whence derives the name for our modern clinics—and went to sleep. If they were lucky, they had a healing dream. If they were luckier, a snake came in the night and bit them—the snake being a symbol for transformation, by virtue of shedding its skin. The luckiest of all received both a dream and a snake-bite.

The use of a couch in classical Freudian analysis stems from this ancient practice. Few Jungians use a couch, and nowadays even some Freudians prefer to sit face to face, but it sometimes appears symbolically in the preamble to dreams ("I am lying on a couch . . ."), indicating that the unconscious has been activated.

The wounded healer dynamic can be schematized by a diagram similar to the one used earlier to illustrate the many lines of communication in a relationship.[100] Only the names are different. The drawing here shows six double-headed arrows, indicating that communication moves in both directions. That makes twelve ways in which information can pass between analyst and analysand. Add one more, the completely unexpected, for a baker's dozen.

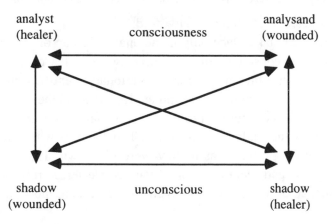

| analyst (healer) | consciousness | analysand (wounded) |
| shadow (wounded) | unconscious | shadow (healer) |

---

[100] Above, page 69.

According to this paradigm, although the analyst is presumed to have become somewhat conscious of his or her own wounds through a personal analysis, they still live a shadowy existence. Which is to say, they don't hurt so much, but they can always be reconstellated by phantoms from the past or by contact with someone whose wounds are similar.

Enter the analysand on his or her knees, hurting but not knowing why. That person's inner healer is in the shadow, potentially available. Various dialogues take place, one at a time or simultaneously, as shown in the diagram. The analysand's wounds are transmitted through the unconscious to the analyst, who experiences, say, a knot in the stomach, or feelings of anxiety. The analyst identifies these symptoms and attempts to reach a conscious understanding of the wounds behind them. One way or another, the analyst's awareness is then passed back to the analysand.

In this model, clearly, the silent unconscious relationship between analyst and analysand is quite as important, in terms of the healing process, as what is actually spoken—and possibly even more so. As James Hillman points out:

> In an analysis, the intimacy grows between two people less through the horizontal connection than through the parallel vertical connections of each within himself. Each listens as much to the effect of the other within and to these inner reactions as to the other. Each takes the other in.[101]

The implications of all this are twofold:

1) Healing can take place only if the analyst has an ongoing relationship with the unconscious, that is, stays aware of his or her shadowy wounds. Otherwise the analyst risks inflationary identification with the healer, in which case both analyst and analysand are in the soup.

2) Analysis is a dangerous profession. An analyst is ever prone to being infected by the analysand's wounds. This happens when you take on somebody else's problems as if they were your own. The thin line between empathy and identification, discussed earlier, is reflected in the high incidence of depression and even suicide among those in the helping professions.

---

[101] *Insearch,* p. 38.

It is now well known that analysis is not a panacea. The mystery is what happens when it works—why some people actually benefit from it. The wounded healer concept does not exhaust the possibilities, but, for want of a better, it makes sense to me.

The Hero's Journey

Although I didn't realize it at the time, the day I entered analysis I embarked on a heroic adventure. To understand what this means involves thinking symbolically or metaphorically rather than literally.

Being crippled is an apt metaphor for those who find themselves in a psychological crisis. Broken in spirit, unable to function in their usual way, they are "on their knees"; they want to pull themselves together, get back on their feet. Meanwhile, they "limp along."

In mythology, the motif of the cripple is everywhere. There is the lame Hephaestus, blacksmith to the gods; the Grail legend's fisher king with a gimpy leg; a string of wounded Mesopotamian kings; Pan with goats' feet; Osiris who lost his penis; Harpocrates, son of Isis and Osiris; Mani, the founder of Manichaeism; the Egyptian god Bes, and so on. Being crippled, blind or otherwise incapacitated is often a sign of chthonic (earthy) wisdom, as in legends of dwarfs and dactyls, and the Cabiri, sons of Hephaestus. On the whole, crippledom is an archetypal motif associated with heroes and those with an unusual fate.

It is a hero's task to do something out of the ordinary. For those in analysis this means trying to understand why they act or react the way they do. Dreams, and often outer life too, take on the flavor of a myth or a fairy tale. There are wicked witches (negative mother) and fairy godmothers (positive mother); wizards and elves, demons and wise old men (aspects of the father); helpful animals (instincts) to guide one through the forest of daily life. There are rolling balls and skeins of thread (markers on the way); magic hats and cloaks (attitudes); thorns and needles that prick (projections); giants (complexes) that knock you off your feet (standpoint); princesses (feminine energy) held captive in towers and princes (masculine energy) scaling mountains to rescue them.

That's just for starters. As a matter of fact, I have never come across a motif in a dream that could not also be found in a myth, legend or fairy tale. This is one of the best-kept secrets of psychological development: others have been through the same tortuous trials. And some of them have even survived.

A sword-fight in a dream may reflect the cut-and-thrust of an encounter with your boss; the thorn hedge that protects a sleeping beauty is the prickly animus who keeps lovers at bay; the ravishing vixen who lures you to bed may be a false bride; the secretary guarding the photocopier is a witch in high heels; an outworn conscious attitude is a sickly old king; an absent queen reflects lack of feeling; a quarrelsome royal couple is a conflict between masculine and feminine, ego and anima/animus; nightmares of burglars breaking in suggest shadow sides of oneself demanding recognition; and on and on.

Like the Dummling or youngest brother in many fairy tales, it is appropriate to be naive about the unconscious and what it holds. This actually works in one's favor, since accomplishing some of the tasks required of us will only be possible if we suspend a rational way of looking at things. The Dummling represents an aspect of the individual psyche that has not been coerced by collective pressures. We all had it at first, and still do, buried under the accretions of daily life: a virgin innocence unhobbled by hard knocks; fresh, spontaneous and not yet fixed in rigid patterns; a time when the border between fantasy and reality was permeable. That openness to the unknown is an important element in the struggle to discover our own individual truth.

The goal is to find the treasure, the ring, the golden egg, the elixir of life. Psychologically these all come to the same thing: oneself—one's true feelings and unique potential. This pursuit, by many other names, is a time-honored tradition. It differs greatly in detail, but the patterns are well known; only names, times and places change.

Symbolically, the hero's journey is a round, as illustrated opposite.[102] Among other things, it involves a dangerous trial of some kind, psychologically analogous, writes Jung, to "the attempt to free ego-conscious-

---

[102] Adapted from Joseph Campbell, *The Hero with a Thousand Faces*, p. 245.

ness from the deadly grip of the unconscious."[103] It is a motif represented by imprisonment, crucifixion, dismemberment, abduction—the kind of experience weathered by sun-gods and other heroes since time immemorial: Gilgamesh, Osiris, Christ, Dante, Odysseus, Aeneas, as well as Pinocchio, and Dorothy in *The Wizard of Oz*. In the language of the mystics it is called the dark night of the soul. In everyday life, we know it as a feeling of despair and a desire to hide under the covers.

CALL TO ADVENTURE

Typically, in myth and legend, the hero journeys by ship or braves dark forests, burning deserts, ice fields, etc. He fights a sea monster or dragon, is swallowed, struggles against being bitten or crushed to death, and having arrived inside the belly of the whale, like Jonah, seeks the vital organ and cuts it off, thereby winning release. Eventually the hero must return to his beginnings and bear witness.

The night sea journey myths, an important subset of these hero tales, derive from the perceived behavior of the sun, which, in Jung's lyrical

---

[103] *Symbols of Transformation*, CW 5, par. 539.

image, "sails over the sea like an immortal god who every evening is immersed in the maternal waters and is born anew in the morning."[104] The sun going down, analogous to the loss of energy in a depression, is thus the necessary prelude to rebirth. Cleansed in the healing waters, the ego lives again. Or, in another mythological image, it rises from the ashes, like the phoenix.

Psychologically, the whale-dragon-monster is the unconscious, and in particular the parental complexes. The battles and suffering that take place during the night sea journey symbolize the heroic attempt to assimilate unconscious contents instead of being overwhelmed by them. Symbolically, the vital organ that must be severed is the umbilical cord, the regressive tie to the past. The potential result is the release of energy—the sun on a new day—that has hitherto been tied up with the complexes.

The hero is the one who conquers the dragon, not the one devoured by it. Also, as Jung writes:

> He is no hero who never met the dragon, or who, if he once saw it, declared afterwards that he saw nothing. Equally, only one who has risked the fight with the dragon and is not overcome by it wins the hoard, the "treasure hard to attain." He alone has a genuine claim to self-confidence, for he has faced the dark ground of his self and thereby has gained . . . . an inner certainty which makes him capable of self-reliance.[105]

Few choose the hero's journey. Who would willingly leave the comfort of home and hearth for a whale's belly? Who would want to face dragons? But when something in us demands the journey we are obliged to live it out whether we like it or not.

Analysts cannot save people from the hazards to be faced, nor should they even try. What nature has ordained, let no one interfere with. The hero's journey is an inner imperative that must be allowed to run its course. The most analysts can do is to accompany their charges and alert them to some dangers along the way.

---

[104] Ibid., par. 306.
[105] *Mysterium Coniunctionis,* CW 14, par. 756.

The Importance of Dreams

I never had any dreams before I went into analysis. At least I never remembered them. Well, that's not quite true. When I was six I fell asleep on the toilet and dreamed God came and told me everything would be fine. And I vaguely recall other childhood dreams of magical gardens peopled with elves and fairies.

My first degree was in mathematics and physics. Dreams were not on the curriculum. Then I studied journalism. As a cub reporter, I covered local political speeches. They were full of dreams, but of another kind. Even when I returned to university to study literature and philosophy, I never heard it suggested that dreams might be important.

According to research into the physiology of sleep, we all dream several times a night, shown by so-called REM phenomena—rapid eye movements. People deprived of the level of sleep at which dreams occur soon become anxious and irritable. These experiments, while silent about the content or meaning of dreams, suggest they have an important biological function. Jung went further: he believed that the purpose of dreams was to monitor and regulate the flow of energy in the psyche.

As an adult, then, I must have had dreams, but for lack of attention they died in the water. Why would I be interested in dreams anyway? They happen at night and have nothing to do with me. That's what I thought until I woke up one morning with a dream that shook me to the core. And I have seldom had a dreamless night since.

An initial dream, the first one brought to an analytic session, is of special significance because it often shows both the underlying factors responsible for bringing a person into analysis and the essential psychological problems that need to be worked through. These may only be apparent in hindsight; perhaps not until years later is that first dream's symbolic content recognized for what it meant at the time. But it always carries a numinosity, a particular fascination or feeling quality, that cannot be denied. One keeps coming back to it as a reference point.

My own initial dream was of a bouncing ball. I was on a street in the center of a deserted city, surrounded by cavernous buildings. I was tossing a ball between the buildings, from one side to another. It kept getting away from me; I could not pin it down. I woke up in a cold sweat, terrified, sobbing uncontrollably. From this distance it seems quite innocuous. At the time it blew my whole world apart.

It was my introduction to the reality of the psyche, a kind of initiation—a baptism by fire. I did not know that something could be going on in me without me being aware of it. I was a child of the Enlightenment. Science, reason and logic were the credos I lived by. I believed that will power could accomplish anything. "Where there's a will there's a way." My bouncing ball dream came in the midst of a mighty conflict which I had a will to solve but no way. I kept thinking I could deal with it by myself. My reaction to the dream killed that illusion.

Jung describes dreams as fragments of involuntary psychic activity, just conscious enough to be reproducible in the waking state. They are self-portraits, symbolic statements of what is going on in the personality from the point of view of the unconscious.

Knowledge of oneself is a result of looking in two directions at once. In order to know ourselves we need both relationships with other people and the mirror of the unconscious. Dreams provide that mirror.

Dreams are independent, spontaneous manifestations of the unconscious. Their message seldom coincides with the tendencies of the conscious mind. They not only fail to obey our will, but often stand in flagrant opposition to our conscious attitudes and intentions. They are not more important than what goes on during the day, but they are helpful comments on our outer existence.

Freud's view was that dreams have an essentially wish-fulfilling and sleep-preserving function. Jung acknowledged this to be true in some cases but focused on the prominent role dreams play in the self-regulation of the psyche. He suggested that their main function was to compensate conscious attitudes—to call attention to different points of view—and in so doing to produce an adjustment in the ego-personality.

Compensation is a process aimed at establishing or maintaining balance in the psyche. If the conscious attitude is too one-sided, the dream takes the opposite tack; if the conscious attitude is more or less appropriate, the dream seems satisfied with pointing out minor variations; and if the conscious attitude is entirely adequate, then the dream may even coincide with and support it.

Dreams have a compensatory function in that they reveal aspects of the personality that are not normally conscious; they disclose unconscious motivations operating in relationships and they present new points of view in conflict situations.

Jung also emphasized the prospective or purposive function of dreams, which means that in many cases their symbolic content outlines the solution of a conscious conflict. This is in line with his view of neurosis as purposeful: the aim of dreams is to present to consciousness the information needed to restore the psyche to a healthy balance.

If that is true, if dreams are really that important, then why are they so difficult to understand? Jung's enigmatic answer is that "the dream is a natural occurrence, and . . . nature shows no inclination to offer her fruits gratis or according to human expectations."[106]

It takes hard work to understand dreams. We aren't used to their symbolic language. The combination of ideas in dreams is essentially fantastic and irrational; images are linked together in a way that is often quite foreign to a linear way of thinking. At first sight they seldom make sense, and often at second sight too. The language of dreams certainly takes some getting used to. One of my more memorable dreams was of a spider on skis, balanced on a razor blade, racing down an Alpine slope. So, the unconscious has a sense of humor.

According to Jung, a dream is an interior drama. The dreamer is the stage, the scene, the director, the author, the actors, the audience and the critic. The dream *is* the dreamer. Each element in a dream refers to an aspect of the dreamer's own personality, which means that the people in our dreams are personifications of our complexes. More: dreams show our complexes at work in determining our attitudes, which are in turn responsible for much of our behavior.

---

[106] "On the Nature of Dreams," *The Structure and Dynamics of the Psyche,* CW 8, par. 560.

Doing the work required to understand the message of a particular dream, or a series with similar motifs, is one of the best ways to depotentiate the complexes because through this focused attention we establish a conscious relationship to them. However, our own dreams are particularly difficult to understand because our blind spots—our complexes—always get in the way to some extent. Even Jung, after working on thousands of his own dreams over a period of fifty years, confessed to this frustration. A rule of thumb is that if you think you understand a dream right off the bat, you've missed the point.

Contrary to popular belief, it is virtually impossible to interpret a dream without the dreamer's cooperation. You need a thorough knowledge of both the context—the outer situation at the time of the dream—and the dreamer's conscious attitude. These, and personal associations to the images in the dream, can only come from the dreamer. If the essential purpose of a dream is to compensate conscious attitudes, you have to know what these are or the dream will forever remain a mystery.

The exception to this is archetypal dreams. These are distinguished by their impersonal nature and the presence of symbolic images and motifs common to myths and religions all over the world. They commonly appear at times of emotional crisis, when one is experiencing a situation that involves a more or less universal human problem. They also tend to occur at times when a new adjustment or change in the conscious attitude is imperative, particularly at periods of transition from one stage of life to another, such as puberty, marriage and midlife.

In this category are dreams of natural disasters: tornadoes, earthquakes, hurricanes and other catastrophic, end-of-the-world images. Only the psychologically naive take these to the streets proclaiming an impending apocalypse.[107] The rest of us look to ourselves. What earth-shattering change is afoot in me? What is rocking my life? What is there

---

[107] There is anecdotal evidence that dreams may foretell disasters in the outside world—in line with ESP and synchronistic experiences that suggest the unconscious moves rather freely through time and space—but this cannot be known at the time of the dream. Hence it is wise to take them personally. See David E. Schoen, *Divine Tempest: The Hurricane As a Psychic Phenomenon*, pp. 59ff.

about my attitude that the unconscious is unhappy with?

There is no fixed meaning to symbols or motifs in dreams, no valid interpretation that is independent of the psychology and life situation of the dreamer. Thus routine recipes and definitions such as those found in traditional dream "dictionaries" are of no value whatever. Nor are exercises aimed at controlling or manipulating the content of dreams. There is no convincing evidence that this is possible, nor would it be desirable even if it were, for one would thereby lose valuable information about oneself that is not available otherwise.

Many dreams have a classic dramatic structure. There is an *exposition* (place, time and characters), which shows the initial situation of the dreamer. In the second phase there is *action,* a development in the plot. The third phase is the culmination or *climax*—a decisive event. The final phase is the *lysis,* the result or solution of the action in the dream. It is often helpful to look at the lysis as showing where the dreamer's energy wants to go. Where there is no lysis, no solution is in sight.

The best way to work on one's dreams is in a dialogue with another person, preferably someone trained to look at dreams objectively and therefore less likely to project his or her own psychology onto their images. Of course, even some knowledge of one's own complexes is no guarantee against projection, but without training of some kind both parties are whistling in the dark.

The first step in working with dreams is to get the dreamer's personal associations to all the images in it. If there is a tree, say, or a rug or a snake or apple, it is important to determine what these mean in the experience of the dreamer. This takes the form of circumambulating the image, which means staying close to it: "What does an elephant mean to you?" . . . "What else?" . . . "And what else?" This is quite different from the traditional Freudian method of free association, which may eventually get to the complex but miss the significance of the image.

On top of personal associations to dream images there are often relevant amplifications—what trees or rugs or snakes or apples have meant to other people in other cultures at other times. A knowledge of archetypal images and motifs serves to broaden conscious awareness by bring-

ing in material that is not personally known but is present in the unconscious as part of everyone's psychic heritage.

Albert, forty-something, brings me this dream:

> I'm in a room. There's shit everywhere. I'm slipping and sliding in it.
> Then I'm on a balcony high above the street. Like a telescope, my eye
> zooms in on a school of fish wriggling through a stream of traffic. The fish
> scales sparkle in the sun. I go looking for my rod and reel.

"As a teenager," he says, "I used to go fishing in the hills of Nova
Scotia, tramping the creeks and streams, bringing home ten- and twelve-
inch brook trout for my mother to cook. They were fun to catch and good
to eat. But I haven't been fishing for years. What does it mean?"

I stare at the wall while my mind buzzes. Broadly speaking, fish in
dreams represent contents of the unconscious, but that isn't saying much
because almost everything does too. More importantly, fish and fishing
symbolism commonly appear when something unconscious is within
reach and needs to be brought to consciousness—reeled in, so to speak.

I have had many dreams myself about fish, and when I was training I
wrote a paper on them. Here are some things I learned:

The yang-yin, male-female polarity is symbolized in Chinese philosophy as two fish: a black one with a white eye, a white one with a black
eye. Together, in a round, they stand for wholeness.

The wounded fisher king in the Grail legend is sick in body and soul
until redeemed by the hero who asks the right question: "Who does the
Grail serve?"—that is, what does it mean to me?

In alchemy the fish is a symbol of both the *prima materia,* the beginning, and the *lapis,* the highest goal, of the seven-stage opus leading to
transformation.

In the Talmud the Messiah is called Dag (fish); His second coming is
to be in the conjunction of Saturn and Jupiter in Pisces, astrological sign
of the two fishes.

The length of a fish is approximately equal to eighteen times the di-
ameter of its eye.

The anima commonly appears in a man's dreams as a mermaid, indicating her close connection with the sea of the unconscious.

Fish frequently turn up in fairy tales as bringers of gifts and helpers in the search for treasure, as in Grimm's "The Sea-Hare."

Jung's book *Aion* has a substantial section on the fish as a symbol of Christ (himself a symbol of the Self), where the fish seems to stand for redemption through bodily suffering—as opposed to birds, which have more to do with spiritual transformation. Elsewhere Jung writes:

> The fish in dreams occasionally signifies the unborn child, because the child before its birth lives in the water like a fish; similarly, when the sun sinks into the seas, it becomes child and fish at once. The fish is therefore a symbol of renewal and rebirth.[108]

With some of this in mind I am not entirely at sea with Albert's dream. He is above the hurly-burly of everyday life (inflation). He sees possibilities but they aren't yet clear (shadowy intuition). And he's still in shit, which means there are more shadow things to be worked on. His personal association with adolescence points to something about those early years that he needs to assimilate, and the fish scales sparkling in the sun suggest to me the potential for this to become conscious.

Should I tell Albert what I know and what I think?

Jung said it makes little difference that the analyst understands what is going on in the unconscious; the important thing is that the analysand understands. In terms of dreams, for instance, there is always the danger that the analyst will step in with a preconceived opinion. It may be on the mark, but such a truth reaches only the head. Understanding in analysis aims more at the heart and is only worthwhile if it comes as "an agreement which is the fruit of joint reflection."[109] Anything else falls into the category of suggestion, a kind of magic that works in the dark and makes no ethical demands.

"It's a mystery to me," I shrug. "Go home. Think fish. Read about them. Draw them. Fashion images in clay. Go out and try to catch a few. See what gets hooked."

---

[108] *Symbols of Transformation,* CW 5, par. 290.
[109] "The Practical Use of Dream-Analysis," *The Practice of Psychotherapy,* CW 16, pars. 314ff.

Garnering personal and archetypal associations to a dream, and its context in the dreamer's waking life, is a relatively simple, almost mechanical procedure. It is necessary, but only preparation for the real work—the actual interpretation of the dream and what it is saying about the dreamer's conscious attitudes. This is an exacting task and an experience so intimate that the interpretation of any particular dream is really only valid for the two persons working on it.

In general, dreams may be interpreted on a subjective or an objective level, and sometimes both are relevant. The former approach considers a dream strictly in terms of the dreamer's own psychology. If a person I know appears in my dream, the focus is not on that actual person but on him or her as an image or symbol of projected unconscious contents. Where I have a vital connection with that person, however, an objective interpretation may be more to the point; the dream may be commenting on a significant aspect of our relationship.

In either case, the image of the other person derives from my own psychology. But whether a subjective or objective approach is more valid, or some balance in between, has to be determined from the context of the dream and the personal associations. That is the work of analysis.

Dreams invariably have more than one meaning. Ten analysts can look at a dream and come up with ten different interpretations, depending on their typology and their own complexes. That is why there is no valid interpretation without dialogue, and why the dreamer must have the final say. What "clicks" for the dreamer is "right"—but only for the moment, because subsequent events and later dreams often throw new light on previous interpretations.

Active Imagination

Other than dreams, the practice of active imagination is a useful activity for tracking what is going on the unconscious. It is not generally recommended for those not in analysis, simply because what comes up may not have a pretty face and can in fact be quite scary. Also, perhaps fortunately, active imagination is not easy to get into.

Active imagination can be painting or music, dance, working in clay, writing—whatever you feel like doing. You follow the energy where it wants to go. The less formal training you have the better, because the trained mind inhibits freedom of expression. It is a way of giving the unconscious an outlet, so you don't explode. It is also another kind of container; instead of dumping your affect on other people you keep it to yourself—you take responsibility for what's yours.

Personally, I was unable to do active imagination until my analyst suggested some simple steps. The first of these was to overcome my fear of a blank sheet of paper.

"Take a page of a newspaper," he said. "Lay a plate on it. Draw an outline of the plate with a crayon or a colored pencil or a paint brush. Look at what you made. Think about it. Now do something inside the circle. You can do anything you want—anything. It's up to you."

This was wily advice because, as I later learned, any circular image is in effect a mandala, and mandalas are traditionally, that is to say archetypally, containers of the mystery. At the time I certainly needed a container, and everything was a mystery to me.

Before long my walls were covered with images of me. I graduated from colorful mandalas to stick figures, and then reflections of a mood. I moved on from newspaper to cardboard to good quality bond. I used whatever came to hand: pencils, pen, paint, felt-tipped markers, fingers, toes. My drawings and paintings were crude depictions of whatever was going on in me when I did them. They had no style or technique and people who came to visit my hole-in-the-wall apartment looked askance. When I come across them now they do seem grotesque, but at the time I loved them and my soul rejoiced.

Jung himself pioneered active imagination by painting and writing his dreams and fantasies. In fact, he pinpointed it as fundamental both to his formulation of the anima/animus concept and to the importance of personifying unconscious contents:[110]

> When I was writing down these fantasies, I once asked myself, "What am I really doing? Certainly this has nothing to do with science. But then what

---

[110] *Memories, Dreams, Reflections*, pp. 210f.

is it?" Whereupon a voice within said, "It is art." I was astonished. It had never entered my head that what I was writing had any connection with art. Then I thought, "Perhaps my unconscious is forming a personality that is not me, but which is insisting on coming through to expression." I knew for a certainty that the voice had come from a woman . . . . a living figure within my mind.

Jung said very emphatically to this voice that his fantasies had nothing to do with art, and he felt a great inner resistance.

Then came the next assault, and again the same assertion: "That is art." This time I caught her and said, "No, it is not art! On the contrary, it is nature," and prepared myself for an argument. When nothing of the sort occurred, I reflected that the "woman within me" did not have the speech centres I had. And so I suggested that she use mine. She did so and came through with a long statement.

Intrigued by the fact that a woman could interfere with him from within, Jung concluded that she must be his "soul," in the primitive sense, and he began to speculate on the reasons why the name "anima" was traditionally given to the soul. Why was it thought of as feminine?

Later I came to see that this inner feminine figure plays a typical, or archetypical, role in the unconscious of a man, and I called her the "anima." The corresponding figure in a woman I called the "animus."

Jung also realized that by personifying that inner voice he was less likely to be seduced into believing he was something he wasn't. In effect, he was writing letters to his anima, a part of himself with a viewpoint different from his conscious one. And by writing out his fantasies, he gave her no chance "to twist them into intrigues":

If I had taken these fantasies of the unconscious as art, they would have carried no more conviction than visual perceptions, as if I were watching a movie. I would have felt no moral obligation towards them. The anima might then have easily seduced me into believing that I was a misunderstood artist, and that my so-called artistic nature gave me the right to neglect reality. If I had followed her voice, she would in all probability have said to me one day, "Do you imagine the nonsense you're engaged in is really art? Not a bit." Thus the insinuations of the anima, the mouthpiece of the unconscious, can utterly destroy a man.

The object of active imagination, then, is to give a voice to sides of the personality that one is ordinarily not aware of—to establish a line of communication between consciousness and the unconscious. It is not necessary to interpret the material, to figure out what it "means." You do it and you live with it. Something goes on between you and what you create, and it doesn't need to be put into words to be effective.

Once I started painting and drawing, I stopped feeling sorry for myself. I also stopped thinking about what my lover might be doing when I wasn't around. I focused on myself and how I felt. Whenever I got into a mood, I captured it with a concrete image or had a talk with my inner woman. Instead of accusing others of causing my heartache, I asked my heart why it ached. Then I drew or wrote an answer.

One of my first sketches showed a woman tied to a rock—the feminine fused with matter. Psychologically this relates to the Eve stage of anima development: being mother-bound. I described it to my analyst as my mountain-anima, because it reminded me of fairy tales where the princess is imprisoned on top of a mountain.

"A real sweetheart," he observed. "But she has no feet."
I took this to mean that my feelings weren't grounded.

One of my early paintings showed a man with head bent, under a black cloud. A bird fluttered above him.

"What kind of bird is that?" asked my analyst.

I considered. "A raven comes to mind." I'm fond of Edgar Allan Poe.

"In alchemy," said my analyst, "the raven is a symbol for the *nigredo* —melancholy, an affliction of the soul, confusion, depression."

That took me to a mournful passage in Kafka's *Diaries*. In the next session I read it to my analyst:

> I don't believe people exist whose inner plight resembles mine; still, it is possible for me to imagine such people—but that the secret raven forever flaps about their heads as it does about mine, even to imagine that is impossible.[111]

"Yes, the 'poor me' syndrome," he said, "heavily laced with inflation, the feeling of being special—nobody suffers as much as you do. As if depression played favorites."

I swallowed that and worked on it.

Every time I went to analysis I took something new. Once I made a pair of clay penises. One was tiny, a shriveled little thing; the other was erect and powerful. We set them up between us.

"Bud Abbott and Lou Costello?" said my analyst.

"David and Goliath?" I suggested. "Mutt and Jeff?"

Writing is for many the most satisfying form of active imagination. You have a dialogue with what's going on inside. You conjure up an image of what you're feeling, personify it and talk to it, then you listen to what it says back. You write this down to make it real, to give it substance. That's the difference between active imagination and a daydream. If you don't fix it in time and space, it's pie in the sky.

For years I have talked regularly with my anima. From not knowing I had a soul, I came to realize I was lost without one. Not all of this was put on my inner woman, but enough. Similar to Jung's experience, I first became aware of her as a phantom mate who wanted attention; she put me in a bad mood when she didn't get it. So we talked and fought and

---

[111] *The Diaries of Franz Kafka, 1914-1923*, p. 195.

made up, and then did it all again, and again and again. Over time we have established a workable relationship—which means I take what she says to heart and do what I can to make my reality acceptable to us both.

My anima has had many names, the latest being Rachel. As muse and spirited interlocutor, she has been a great help in both my life and my writing. All the same, she has a mind of her own and sometimes pops up uninvited. Here is an exchange that took place when I was writing *Dear Gladys* and trying to get a handle on the creative process:[112]

Nobody knows what goes on when you write a book. There are theories, but nobody really *knows*. The only sure thing is that there are as many different ways to write as there are writers.

Some say they till the ground, plant the seed and watch it grow. For me it's like assembling a patchwork quilt. My computer is little more than a sewing machine. I have the patches; it's the needles that give me a hard time.

Jung had something to say on the subject. Of course he didn't *know* either, but he had some ideas. In volume 17 of his Collected Works there are several essays that deal particularly with the creative way. One is on James Joyce, one is on Picasso; the others are more general.

Here is Jung's basic standpoint:

The practice of art is a psychological activity and, as such, can be approached from a psychological angle. Considered in this light, art, like any other human activity deriving from psychic motives, is a proper subject for psychology. This statement, however, involves a very definite limitation of the psychological viewpoint when we come to apply it in practice. Only that aspect of art which consists in the process of artistic creation can be a subject for psychological study, but not that which constitutes its essential nature. The question of what art is in itself can never be answered by the psychologist, but must be approached from the side of aesthetics.[113]

"Huh!" said Rachel. "Already he's hedging."

Ah, she's been hiding in the weeds; sniping at the elephants, I bet.

"No, he's not," I said. "He's laying down ground rules. He's setting limits to what psychology can meaningfully say about art."

"Sure," nodded Rachel, "that's his way. He'll go on like that for a hun-

---

[112] *Dear Gladys* is book 2 of *The Survival Papers* (above, p. 58, note 45).

[113] "On the Relation of Analytical Psychology to Poetry," *The Spirit in Man, Art, and Literature,* CW 17, par. 97.

dred pages and at the end, in the very last paragraph, he'll admit he knows nothing at all."

I was surprised at Rachel's scorn.

"Look," I said, "the way I understand it, Jung is saying that the process of creating is a legitimate subject for psychological speculation. But psychology can't determine whether the end result is art or not. That depends on contemporary taste. Van Gogh, for instance, died poor. Today his work fetches millions. Kafka was not appreciated in his lifetime. Now his work is hailed as a milestone in the history of modern literature."

"So?" said Rachel. "It all comes down to we know what we like."

"Oh? Why do we like what we like?"

"Well," said Rachel, "because it's art."

This would go nowhere.

"Okay," I agreed. "Never mind all the factors involved in what we like, the things we call art. But how did what we like, or not, come to be? Think about that. Why did Michelangelo sweat his guts out painting the Sistine Chapel on his back? Where did Leonardo da Vinci get the idea for flying machines 400 years before they existed? What inspired Jackson Pollock to throw paint at canvas when nobody else did? What possessed Picasso?"

Rachel took that in. I gave her another example, closer to home.

"Where did the idea to write about Norman come from? Don't ask if he's real or not, or if it's art. How did I come to put energy into his story? I'd rather play snooker any day, or stare at the wall. But here I am, glued to the computer. Who or what is responsible?"

Rachel knit her brow. A wisp of hair fluttered on her cheek. She brushed it back. A sexy woman in the prime of life. I love her, I thought.

"God?" she offered.

Good grief! What does she have between her ears? God used to be an okay explanation for *everything*. In this day and age, God is either a minor player or not in the game at all.

I shook my head. "I hardly think so."

And lucky too. If I did, I'd be out there with the rest of them, touting the Word. I'd have a program on prime-time teevee, turning lead into gold. I'd have a theme park dedicated to my mother. People who couldn't afford to would send me money. I'd put it in the bank and feel righteous. I'd be bigger than my boots, a goner.

"God, if he exists," I said, "has more important things to do. At least I hope so. Don't you agree?"

Rachel inclined her head.

"Jung has an explanation," I said. "Listen to this":

The unborn work in the psyche of the artist is a force of nature that achieves its end either with tyrannical might or with the subtle cunning of nature herself, quite regardless of the personal fate of the man who is its vehicle. The creative urge lives and grows in him like a tree in the earth from which it draws its nourishment. We would do well, therefore, to think of the creative process as a living thing implanted in the human psyche.[114]

"God, nature, what's the difference?" said Rachel.
"Wait, I didn't finish."

In the language of analytical psychology this living thing is an *autonomous complex*. It is a split-off portion of the psyche, which leads a life of its own outside the hierarchy of consciousness. Depending on its energy charge, it may appear either as a mere disturbance of conscious activities or as a supraordinate authority which can harness the ego to its purpose.[115]

"Do you see? It's a complex that drives people to create."
Rachel found that hard to swallow.
"So artists are neurotic, is that it? Art is the result of neurosis?"
I gnashed my teeth.
"No, you misunderstand the nature of a complex. It's a feeling-toned idea that gets you by the throat. It's only neurotic when it gets in the way. You can be stimulated to create because of a complex, but what you produce still has to be shaped. You can't do that unless you have some distance from the complex. There are creative people who would do better work if they weren't so neurotic. And there are neurotics whose creativity is locked in the closet. Complexes are the key. Understand your complexes and it's a whole new ball game."
Rachel mused about that.
"Where do I fit in?"
"You're the bridge to what's going on in me. You mediate the contents of my unconscious. Without you I'd have nothing to work with. Thanks to you, it wells up in me. It's all there, I can see it. But it has to be given an appropriate form. That's my job."
"I think I understand," said Rachel. "But what starts the creative process? What sparks the complex?"
I leaned back. I could speak of archetypes, the collective unconscious. I could give examples from fairy tales, mythology and religion. I could cite

---

[114] Ibid., par. 115.
[115] Ibid.

literature from all over the world. Yes, I could babble on for a hundred pages and come back to square one.

"I don't know," I said. "It's a mystery to me."

Rachel smiled. "That's what I said in the first place—*God.*"

Active imagination can also take the form of dreaming a dream on— you pick up the action at the end of a dream and imagine what might happen next. This is an excellent way to learn more about your complexes, but to do it successfully, you have to still your sceptical, rational mind, which will call it nonsense and say you made it all up. And of course you did—but who is "you"? Nonsense it may seem, but wisdom it may hold. As noted earlier, many writers actually make use of this method (though not always consciously) in dramatizing the interaction of their complexes—as did I in the above dialogue with Rachel.

Jung emphasized that for active imagination to be psychologically useful, which is to say transformative, one has to move beyond a merely aesthetic appreciation of the action or images and take an ethical stand toward them—relate them to what is happening in your life, and judge their meaning in that context:

> As a rule there is a marked tendency simply to enjoy this interior entertainment and to leave it at that. Then, of course, there is no real progress but only endless variations on the same theme, which is not the point of the exercise at all. . . . If the observer understands that his own drama is being performed on this inner stage, he cannot remain indifferent to the plot and its dénouement. He will notice, as the actors appear one by one and the plot thickens, that they all have some purposeful relationship to his conscious situation, that he is being addressed by the unconscious and that *it* causes these fantasy-images to appear before him.[116]

Recognizing your own involvement, you are then obliged to enter into the process with your personal reactions, just as if you were one of the fantasy figures—as if the drama being enacted were real. As indeed it is, for psychic facts are quite as real as table-tops. If you place yourself in the drama as you really are, not only does it gain in actuality but you also

---

[116] *Mysterium Coniunctionis,* CW 14, par. 706.

create, by your criticism of the fantasy, an effective counterbalance to its tendency to get out of hand. What you are experiencing, after all, is an encounter with the unconscious, the sine qua non of the transcendent function and another step on the path of individuation.

As I was writing this, I read in the newspaper that a newly appointed Lieutenant-Governor of Quebec, provincial representative of the Queen of England, had divulged to reporters that before accepting the honor she conferred with her ancestors. "Because," she said, "they know me." Her candor earned a shrieking headline: **Madame D— talks to the dead!**

The press corps raked her over the coals, questioning her sanity. But of course such a dialogue is a legitimate use of active imagination, good for her and harmless to others. I think the only mistake she made was telling the world; perhaps she lacked a personal container.

For those in analysis, active imagination of one kind or another is good preparation for leaving. You don't stay in therapy forever. When the time comes to stop, it is a useful tool to take away with you.

6

Psychological Development

*The reason why consciousness exists, and why there is an urge to widen
and deepen it, is very simple: without consciousness things go less well.*
— C.G. Jung.

Becoming Conscious

One of Jung's basic beliefs, and arguably his most important message, is
that the purpose of human life is to become conscious. "As far as we can
discern," he writes in later life, "the sole purpose of human existence is
to kindle a light in the darkness of mere being."[117] Part and parcel of this
is achieving a balance, a right harmony, between mind and body, spirit
and instinct. Go too far one way or the other and we become neurotic.
Jung says it in one pithy sentence:

> Too much of the animal distorts the civilized man, too much civilization
> makes sick animals.[118]

The "civilized man" tends to live in his head. He prides himself on a
rational approach to life, and rightly so. We are no longer apes. Thanks to
reason, science and logic, instead of hanging from trees or living in them,
we cut them down to build houses, which we then fill with appliances to
make life easier.

All the same, the more we lose touch with our other side, our instinctual base, the more likely it is that something will happen in us to bring
about a proper balance. This is the basis for Jung's idea of compensation
within the psyche. One way or another, we'll be brought down to earth. It
is just when we think we have everything under control that we are most
apt to fall on our face, and this is especially true when we don't reckon
with the uncivilized, ten-million-year-old animal in us.

That being said, unexamined instinctual behavior is a hallmark of un-

---

[117] *Memories, Dreams, Reflections*, p. 326.
[118] "The Eros Theory," *Two Essays*, CW 7, par. 32.

consciousness and a fundamental characteristic of the undeveloped personality. Through analysis one can become conscious of the instincts and the many ways in which we are slaves to them. But this is not done with a view to giving them boundless freedom. The aim is rather to incorporate them into a purposeful whole.

Jung defined consciousness as "the function or activity which maintains the relation of psychic contents to the ego."[119] In that way he distinguished it conceptually from the psyche itself, which is comprised of both consciousness and the unconscious. Also, although we may speak of ego-consciousness, in Jung's model the ego is not the same thing as consciousness; it is simply the dominant complex of the conscious mind. Of course, in practice we can only become aware of psychic contents by means of the ego; which is to say, the more we know about what's going on in our unconscious, the more conscious we become.

My analyst once said to me: "Think of what you've been, what you are now, and then reflect on what you could be." This is a useful exercise not only for a bird's-eye perspective on where you are on the journey of individuation, but also because it alerts you to what might be missing.

We live in a stream of events. Something new happens to us every day, but most of us are so caught up in routine that we don't even notice. Consciousness is the result of observing and reflecting on events instead of simply reacting to them. Routine especially gets in the way of being conscious. We can sleepwalk through life as long as we stick to the tried and true.

A few years ago I got a taste of what the unconscious can do to wake us up. I had agreed to give a Friday evening lecture and a Saturday seminar in Lafayette, Louisiana. I had mixed feelings about this because I don't like traveling; it interferes with my routine. But I booked my flight three months in advance to get the cheapest fare, and I was packed and ready to go two days before the flight. That too is routine for me and typical of my typology; I pride myself on attention to detail and on being well prepared.

It was an uneventful flight, and late that Friday afternoon I stood out-

---

[119] "Definitions," *Psychological Types,* CW 6, par. 700.

side the Lafayette airport waiting for my pick-up. Nobody came and nobody came. After about half an hour I noticed that the passing cars all had *Indiana* license plates. And there, right in front of me, was a big sign giving directions to the University of Notre Dame. Well, talk about your sinking heart.

Of course I had checked my ticket, and more than once. It said Lafayette, IN, but I thought that meant "in" as opposed to "out"—and I *was* going *in* to Lafayette.

That experience has more than one meaning for me, but at least it is clear that I was blind-sided by my inferior intuition, the possibilities; in this case, that there might be more than one Lafayette in the United States. In fact there are over twenty. Luckily my return ticket took me back to Canada instead of to a Toronto in Texas, South Dakota, Ohio, Maryland, Illinois, Indiana, Iowa or Kansas.

Becoming conscious preeminently involves discriminating between opposites. As noted earlier, the basic opposites are ego-consciousness and the unconscious, so the first hurdle is to acknowledge that there are indeed some things about yourself you're not aware of. Those who cannot do this are doomed forever to skim the surface of life. For those who can admit to another side of themselves, there is then the daunting task of discriminating between a whole range of other opposites—thinking and feeling, masculine and feminine, good and bad, and so on. And then there is the crucial difference between inner and outer, oneself and others; sorting that out can easily take a few years.

Jung describes two distinct ways in which consciousness is enlarged. One is during a moment of high emotional tension involving a situation in the outer world. We feel uneasy for no obvious reason, or strangely attracted to someone, and suddenly we understand what's going on. The other way is what happens in a state of quiet contemplation, where ideas pass before the mind's eye like dream-images. Suddenly there is a flash of association between two apparently disconnected and widely separated thoughts. In each case it is the discharge of energy-tension that produces consciousness. These sudden realizations and flashes of insight are what we commonly experience as revelations.

In Jung's model of the psyche, consciousness is a kind of superstructure based on the unconscious and arising out of it:

> Consciousness does not create itself—it wells up from unknown depths. In childhood it awakens gradually, and all through life it wakes each morning out of the depths of sleep from an unconscious condition. It is like a child that is born daily out of the primordial womb of the unconscious. . . . It is not only influenced by the unconscious but continually emerges out of it in the form of spontaneous ideas and sudden flashes of thought.[120]

Elsewhere he uses a different metaphor:

> In the child, consciousness rises out of the depths of unconscious psychic life, at first like separate islands, which gradually unite to form a "continent," a continuous land-mass of consciousness. Progressive mental development means, in effect, extension of consciousness.[121]

A child lives in a state of oneness with its primary care-giver. There is little separation between subject and object. As the growing child assimilates experience and develops personal boundaries—a sense of self separate from the outside world—so the ego comes into being. There is a recognizable sense of personal identity, an "I am." This goes on in fits and starts, until at some point you have this metaphorical "land-mass of consciousness," surrounded by the waters of the unconscious.

The first half of life generally involves this developmental process. If we get decent mirroring in the early years, we stand a good chance of acquiring a healthy ego. But again, this is not the same thing as being conscious. There are lots of take-charge people with very healthy egos—captains of industry, politicians, artists, entrepreneurs and so on—who are still quite unconscious. In fact this would seem to be the rule rather than the exception. You can be a leader, run things like a clock and manage others well. But if you don't take the time to introspect, to question who you are without your external trappings, you can't claim to be conscious.

Mature consciousness, according to Jung, is dependent on a working relationship between a strong but flexible ego and the Self, regulating center of the psyche. For that to happen one has to acknowledge that the ego is not in charge. This is not a natural process; it is *contra naturam,*

---

[120] "The Psychology of Eastern Meditation," *Psychology and Religion,* CW 11, par. 935.
[121] "The Development of Personality," *The Development of Personality,* CW 17, par. 326.

against nature, a major shift in perspective, like the difference between thinking the earth is the center of the solar system and then learning that the sun is. Bam! This generally doesn't happen until later in life, when you look back on your experience and realize there was more going on than you knew. Ergo, something other than "you" was pulling the strings.

Becoming conscious, then, is not a one-time thing; it is a continuous process, *by* the ego, of assimilating what was previously unknown *to* the ego. It involves a progressive understanding of why we do what we do. And a major step is to become aware of the many ways we're influenced by unconscious aspects of ourselves, which is to say, our complexes.

Being conscious also has little to do with the accumulation of knowledge or academic degrees. It is rather a function of how much we know about ourselves. And although no one is ever totally unconscious, on the other hand we can only ever be relatively more conscious—compared to what we were before.

Jung visualized the unconscious as an ocean, because both are inexhaustible. Freud saw the unconscious, or subconscious, as little more than a garbage can of fantasies and emotions that were active when we were children and then were repressed or forgotten. Jung accepted that for a while. He was an early champion of Freud's theories, but in the end Freud's dogma just didn't accord with Jung's experience. Jung came to believe instead that the unconscious also includes contents we never knew were there: things about ourselves (in our personal unconscious), and then, at a deeper level (the collective unconscious), all the varied experiences of the human race, the stuff of myth and religion—a vast historical warehouse. Under the right circumstances, any of this can become conscious. Jung writes:

> Everything of which I know, but of which I am not at the moment thinking; everything of which I was once conscious but have now forgotten; everything perceived by my senses, but not noted by my conscious mind; everything which, involuntarily and without paying attention to it, I feel, think, remember, want, and do; all the future things that are taking shape in me and will sometime come to consciousness: all this is the content of the unconscious.[122]

---

[122] *The Structure and Dynamics of the Psyche,* CW 8, par. 382.

And that is why, in spite of our best efforts, we will always be more or less unconscious.

To my mind, we are forever prisoners of our personal psychology, but if we work on ourselves enough we might make day parole. Or, to use the earlier metaphor, over time we can establish a few beachheads, but there are still all those other islands.

Self-knowledge

In my early life I belonged to a church whose minister put the Ten Commandments on one side and Satan on the other. This is white and that is black, and the devil take you for a wrong choice. He knew his opposites all right; they were cut and dried, with no bridge between. But my experience is that life consists of myriad shades of gray. I now say, know who you are and guide yourself accordingly. The difficult part is knowing who you are.

Most people confuse self-knowledge with knowledge of their conscious ego-personalities. Those with any ego-consciousness at all take it for granted that they know themselves. But the real psychic facts are for the most part hidden. The ego knows only its own contents, which are largely dependent on social factors. Without some knowledge of the unconscious and its contents one cannot claim to know oneself.

The average person knows little about the intricate physiological and anatomical structure of the body, yet we are accustomed to take steps against physical infection. Complexes are just as real, and just as invisible, as germs. Against pervasive unconsciousness we are virtually defenceless, open to all manner of influences and psychic infections. We can guard against the risk of psychic infection only when we know what is attacking us, and how, where and when the attack might come.

Self-knowledge is a matter of getting to know your own individual facts. Theories are of little help, notes Jung:

> The more a theory lays claim to universal validity, the less capable it is of doing justice to the individual facts. Any theory based on experimentation is necessarily *statistical;* it formulates an *ideal average* which abolishes all exceptions at either end of the scale and replaces them by an abstract mean. This mean is quite valid, though it need not necesarily occur in re-

ality. . . . The exceptions at either end, though equally factual, do not appear in the final result at all, since they cancel each other out.[123]

Jung gives this example:

If, for instance, I determine the weight of each stone in a pile of pebbles and get an average weight of five ounces, this tells me very little about the real nature of the pebbles. Anyone who thought, on the basis of these findings, that he could pick up a pebble of five ounces at the first try would be in for a serious disappointment. Indeed, it might well happen that however long he searched he would not find a single pebble weighing exactly five ounces.

. . . . The distinctive thing about real facts, however, is their individuality. Not to put too fine a point on it, one could say that the real picture consists of nothing but exceptions to the rule . . . .

These considerations must be borne in mind whenever there is talk of a theory serving as a guide to self-knowledge. There is and can be no self-knowledge based on theoretical assumptions, for the object of this knowledge is . . . a relative exception and an irregular phenomenon.[124]

Similarly, in the treatment of psychic suffering, Jung always stressed that the so-called scientific knowledge of humankind in general must take second place; the important thing is the particular person. On the one hand the analyst is equipped with statistical truths, and on the other is faced with someone who requires individual understanding. One need not deny the validity of statistics, but the more schematic the treatment, the more resistances it calls up in the patient. The analyst therefore needs to have a kind of two-way thinking: doing one thing while not losing sight of the other.

The recognition that there is an unconscious side of ourselves has fundamentally altered the pursuit of self-knowledge. It is apparent now that we are twofold beings: we have a conscious side we more or less know, and an unconscious side of which we know little but which in all likelihood is no secret to others. When we lack knowledge of our other side, we can do the most terrible things without calling ourselves to account and without ever suspecting what we're doing. Thus we may be baffled

---

[123] "The Undiscovered Self," *Civilization in Transition,* CW 10, par. 493.
[124] Ibid., pars. 493ff.

by how others react to us. The increased self-knowledge that comes about through depth psychology allows us both to remedy our own mistakes and to become more understanding and tolerant of others.

Self-knowledge can have a healing effect on ourselves and our environment, but this seldom happens without a prolonged period of professional analysis. Self-analysis works to the extent that we are alert to the effects of our behavior and willing to learn from them; however, it is limited by our blind-spots—our complexes—and by the silence of others who for one reason or another indulge them. To really get a handle on ourselves we need an honest, objective mirror. Our intimates are rarely that. The unconscious is a rather more unsparing mirror, and analysts are trained to interpret the reflections.

Historically, the triad of repentance, confession and purification from sin have been the conditions of salvation. That has traditionally been the province of religion, and for some it still is, but among unbelievers the role is filled by depth psychology. As far as analysis helps confession, it can bring about a kind of renewal. Again and again, patients dream of analysis as a refreshing and purifying bath, or other symbols of rebirth appear in their dreams and visions. The knowledge of what is going on in their unconscious gives them renewed vitality.

There are many methods and techniques espoused by therapists of different schools, but Jung's view was that technique is not important. What matters is rather the analyst's self-knowledge and continuing attention to his or her own unconscious. Analysis is in fact both a craft and an art. Whatever school an analyst trains in, he or she is obliged to deal in an individual way with what comes in the door. Jung said that when a unique, suffering person was in front of him, he put theory on the shelf and listened. Nor did he insist on analyzing the unconscious. Consistent support of the conscious attitude is often enough to bring about satisfactory results. So long as it does not obtrude itself, Jung felt, the unconscious is best left alone. Depth analysis is like a surgical operation; one should only resort to the knife when other methods have failed.

Nobody can be absolutely right in either the physical sciences or the practice of psychology. The tool with which we interpret what happens in both the material world and the psyche is the psyche itself. The observer's psychological predispositions and hypotheses influence what is observed; matter in the outer world and psyche in the inner are not only objects of investigation, but also subjects. It is a vicious circle with few objective guidelines, and so analysts of any school must be very modest in what they claim to do.

Today there are so many psychological theories that it is hard to be serious about any one. The Freudian and Adlerian schools are only two of the most well known of the depth psychologies. There is the Kleinian school and the Kohutians; there are Reichians, Lacanians, Hillmanians and Mindellians; there are those who work with sand, paint, clay, smells, bumps on the head; others still put their faith in abreaction or hypnosis. That is only in the psychodynamic area. There are also behaviorists, neurologists, physicists, linguists, theologians and philosophers who call themselves psychologists.

In short, psychology is a point of view and no one theory explains everything. At the same time, it is very important that therapists believe in their particular approach, for, as Jung pointed out, it is often *that* one believes, not *what,* which has a curative effect.

That being said, Jung's understanding of the psyche seems to appeal to those who are philosophically minded and function reasonably well in outer life. They have inner conflicts and problems in relationships, which of course they rationalize as much as they can, but on the whole they are no more neurotic than the rest of us. They are grateful to learn about the ubiquitous influence of the unconscious and are open to a mythological and symbolic perspective. Much of this they can find in books. The next step, personal analysis, is best suited for those who have reached the end of their tether and have no place else to go.

Self-knowledge can be the antidote to a pervasive malaise, particularly common in middle age, and a spur to an adventurous inner life—the hero's journey, as described earlier. Understanding yourself is also a matter of asking the right questions, again and again. Do that long enough and the capital-S Self, one's regulating center, is activated.

Marie-Louise von Franz says that having a relationship with the Self is like being in touch with an "instinct of truth." There is an immediate awareness of what is right and true, a truth without reflection:

One reacts rightly without knowing why, it flows through one and one does the right thing. . . . With the help of the instinct of truth, life goes on as a meaningful flow, as a manifestation of the Self.[125]

In practical terms, this comes down to simply *knowing* what is right for oneself. One has a strong instinctive feeling of what should be and what could be. To depart from this leads to error, aberration and illness— and to hiding under the covers.

Personally, I owe my life to depth psychology and to the application of Jung's ideas. Once upon a time I was on my knees. After a few years of analysis I could again walk. One day, perhaps, I will jog, or even run. Meanwhile, I truck along with the elephants.

Personality and Individuation

The process of individuation, becoming conscious of what is truly unique about oneself, is inextricably tied up with individuality and the development of personality. The first step is to differentiate ourselves from those we have admired and imitated. Jung writes about this:

We see every day how people use, or rather abuse, the mechanism of imitation for the purpose of personal differentiation: they are content to ape some eminent personality, some striking characteristic or mode of behaviour, thereby achieving an outward distinction from the circle in which they move. . . . As a rule these specious attempts at individual differentiation stiffen into a pose, and the imitator remains at the same level as he always was, only several degrees more sterile than before.[126]

Now there's a screed. And here's another:

Every man is, in a certain sense, unconsciously a worse man when he is in society than when acting alone. . . . *Any large company of wholly admirable persons has the morality and intelligence of an unwieldy, stupid, and violent animal.* The bigger the organization, the more unavoidable is its immorality and blind stupidity. . . . Society, by automatically stressing all the collective qualities in its individual representatives, puts a premium on mediocrity, on everything that settles down to vegetate in an easy, irresponsible way. Individuality will inevitably be driven to the wall.[127]

---

[125] *Alchemy: An Introduction to the Symbolism and the Psychology,* pp. 172f.
[126] "The Relations Between the Ego and the Unconscious,"*Two Essays,* CW 7, par. 242.
[127] Ibid., par. 240 (emphasis added).

Pretty strong stuff. If you were a government beaurocrat or had a key to a corporate washroom and read that, it might make you cringe, or at least wince. Of course it's pretty unlikely you'd ever read it; you'd be in a meeting or have way more important things to do. At least I did when I worked for Procter & Gamble.

In his autobiography, Jung notes that individuality and group identity are incompatible; you can have one or the other, but not both:

> It is really the individual's task to differentiate himself from all others and stand on his own feet. All collective identities, such as membership in organizations, support of "isms," and so on, interfere with the fulfillment of this task. Such collective identities are crutches for the lame, shields for the timid, beds for the lazy, nurseries for the irresponsible.[128]

However, Jung also made it clear that he did not advise people to become antisocial eccentrics. Always he insisted that one must adapt to reality and not disappear into the unconscious, so to speak. We cannot individuate in a corner; we need the mirrors provided by both the unconscious and other people. Our task is to sort out the reflections.

Personality develops by slow stages throughout life. It is achieved as the fruit of activity coupled with introspection, confidence tempered by a healthy dose of self-doubt. According to one of Jung's several definitions, personality is "the supreme realization of the innate idiosyncrasy of a living being."[129] On the one hand, he says, it is an act of courage flung in the face of life, the affirmation of who one is. On the other hand it involves accepting some universal conditions of existence, such as where we find ourselves on this earth and having a physical body. Personality develops from germs that are almost impossible to discern. It is only our deeds that reveal who we are. As Jung writes:

> At first we do not know what deeds or misdeeds, what destiny, what good and evil we have in us. Only the autumn can show what the spring has sown; only in the evening can we see what the morning began.[130]

---

[128] *Memories, Dreams, Reflections,* p. 342.

[129] "The Development of Personality," *The Development of Personality,* CW 17, par. 289.

[130] Ibid., par. 290.

In the beginning we do not know the limits of our potential, and of course we must also make choices. We are not only individuals; we are also social creatures with responsibilities and commitments. These are the inescapable Janus-faces of life: ourselves and other people. We have only so much energy. What we give to one is not available to the other. We are obliged to choose, and then to live with the consequences.

The twin running mates of personality are individuality and individuation. Individuality refers to the qualities or characteristics that distinguish one person from another. Individuation is a process of differentiation and integration, the aim being to become conscious of one's unique psychological make-up. This is quite different from individualism, which is simply me-first and leads inexorably to alienation from the collective. The individuating person may be obliged to deviate from collective norms, but all the same retains a healthy respect for them. In Jung's felicitous phrase, "Individuation does not shut one out from the world, but gathers the world to itself."[131]

Marie-Louise von Franz, asked to comment on what Jung meant by individuation, said the following:

> Individuation means being yourself, becoming yourself. Nowadays one always uses the cheap word "self-realization," but what one really means is ego-realization. Jung means something quite different. He means the realization of one's own predestined development. That does not always suit the ego, but it is what one intrinsically feels could or should be. We are neurotic when we are not what God meant us to be. Basically, that's what individuation is all about. One lives one's destiny. Then usually one is more humane, less criminal, less destructive to one's environment.[132]

When the persona and the routine of life predominate in the form of convention and tradition—doing the right thing, putting your best foot forward and so on—there is apt to be a destructive outbreak of creative energy. Destruction is the dark side of any energy that is repressed. We are all potentially creative, which is not to say artistic, though some are both. We all have innate gifts. Those who are not involved in exploring

---

[131] "On the Nature of the Psyche," *The Structure and Dynamics of the Psyche,* CW 8, par. 432.
[132] "The Geography of the Soul," interview reprinted in *In Touch,* Summer 1993, p. 12.

their own possibilities, their individual talents, will take their frustration out on others or on themselves. Relationships suffer, health deteriorates. Heart and liver ailments, skin problems, kidney disease, cancer, depression and conflict—these are all potential consequences of undeveloped or unlived life. It is difficult to know whether the latter causes the former, or vice versa, but they have been observed to go together.

There is a famous short story by Leo Tolstoy called "The Death of Ivan Ilyich," in which the dying Ilyich, a petty state functionary, laments his past. In the end Ilyich dies in abject sorrow, with the painful realization that he had lived his life according to other people's values. For all his good intentions—or, and how difficult this was to admit, possibly even because of them—he himself had not lived at all.

What motivates a person to individuate, to develop personality instead of settling for persona? Jung's answer is that it doesn't happen by an act of will, or because someone says it would be useful or advisable:

> Nature has never yet been taken in by well-meaning advice. The only thing that moves nature is causal necessity, and that goes for human nature too. Without necessity nothing budges, the human personality least of all. It is tremendously conservative, not to say torpid. . . . The developing personality obeys no caprice, no command, no insight, only brute necessity; it needs the motivating force of inner or outer fatalities. Any other development would be no better than individualism. . . . [which] is a cheap insult when flung at the natural development of personality.
>
> The words "many are called, but few are chosen" are singularly appropriate here, for the development of personality from the germ-state to full consciousness is at once a charisma and a curse, because its first fruit is the segregation of the single individual from the undifferentiated and unconscious herd. This means isolation, and there is no more comforting word for it. Neither family nor society nor position can save one from this fate, nor yet the most successful adaptation to the environment.[133]

Being alone is relatively easy for introverts. They may lack a vital connection with the outer world but they generally have an active inner life. Extraverts are used to hustle and bustle and find it more difficult to live with just themselves. But whatever one's typology, the great challenge in the development of personality is to find a personal center.

---

[133] "The Development of Personality," *Development of Personality,* CW 17, pars. 293f.

Initially one's center is projected onto the family, a self-contained unit experienced as wholeness. Without it we are apt to feel rootless, at loose ends. Leaving one's family triggers an archetypal motif: the awesome schism between heaven and earth, the primordial parents. That is clearly at work behind the reactions of a child whose parents split up, but it is also constellated when one separates from the collective.

Loneliness feels like one has been abandoned. Mythologically, abandonment is associated with the childhood experience of gods and divine heroes—Zeus, Dionysus, Poseidon, Moses, Romulus and Remus, et al. In fact, the motif is so widespread that Jung describes abandonment as "a necessary condition and not just a concomitant symptom," of the potentially higher consciousness symbolized by images of the child in a person's dreams.[134]

Anyone in the process of becoming independent must detach from his or her origins: mother, family, society. Sometimes this transition happens smoothly. If it does not, the result is twofold: the "poor me" syndrome, characteristic of the regressive longing for dependence, and a psychic experience of a potentially creative nature—the positive side of the divine child archetype: new life, exciting new possibilities. The incompatibility between these two directions generates a conflict that is invariably present in a psychological crisis. This conflict is the price that has to be paid in order to grow up. On the one hand, we long to return to the past; on the other, we are drawn inexorably toward an unknown future.

Initially, this conflict goes hand in hand with the feeling of loneliness, behind which is the archetypal motif of the abandoned child. Thus Jung observes, "Higher consciousness . . . is equivalent to being *all alone in the world.*"[135] In short, personality is a gift that is paid for dearly.

As well, personality cannot develop unless one chooses his or her own way consciously and with moral deliberation. And so to the causal motive mentioned earlier—necessity—we must add conscious moral decision. If the first is lacking, then the alleged development is merely willful acrobatics; if the second, it will become mechanical and sterile.

---

[134] "The Psychology of the Child Archetype," *The Archetypes and the Collective Unconscious,* CW 9i, par. 287.
[135] Ibid., par. 288.

You can make a commitment to go your own way only if you believe that way to be better for you than other, conventional ways of a moral, social, political or religious nature—any of the well-known "isms." Those who adhere to them do not choose their own way; they develop not themselves but a method and a collective mode of life at the cost of their own wholeness.

Moreover, personality is not the prerogative of genius. One may be a genius without being a personality, or the other way around, since everyone has an inborn law of life to answer to. In short, mental prowess is but a minor component of personality, nor is it a significant factor in individuation. Indeed, as noted already, in fairy tales, where so many psychic patterns are illustrated, the one who finds the treasure "hard to attain" is as often as not a Dummling, an innocent fool.

The primary question in speaking of personality, as of individuation, is always, "Do you know who you are? Are you living your own way?" The answer is seldom found without conscious effort, but that is essentially, metaphorically, the treasure the Dummling seeks.

Jung points out that because individuality and the development of personality are deviations not congenial to the collective, historically only a few have dared the adventure, the hero's journey, but these are the ones we now invoke to give us heart:

> [They] are as a rule the legendary heroes of mankind, the very ones who are looked up to, loved, and worshipped, the true sons of God whose names perish not. . . . Their greatness has never lain in their abject submission *to* convention, but, on the contrary, in their deliverance *from* convention. They towered up like mountain peaks above the mass that still clung to its collective fears, its beliefs, laws, and systems, and boldly chose their own way.[136]

From the beginning of recorded time, heroes have been endowed with godlike attributes. Anyone who would turn aside from the beaten path and strike out on the steep unknown was either crazy or possessed by a demon, or possibly a god. Some were coddled, just in case; the unlucky ones were hacked to pieces or burned at the stake.

---

[136] Ibid., par. 298.

Now we have depth psychology. On a collective level we still have heroes—athletes, actors, politicians and the like—and some of these we treat like gods. But we no longer expect of them anything as elusive and differentiated as personality. Individually, however, we have raised our sights. Thanks to Jung we now know that personality, in any substantial use of the term, depends upon a harmonious mix of ego, persona and shadow, in helpful alliance with anima or animus, our contrasexual sides, *plus* a working relationship with something greater, like the Self.

Call it God or the Self, or by any other name, without contact with an inner center we have to depend on will power, which is not enough to save us from ourselves, nor to make a personality out of a sow's ear.

Simply and naturally, by virtue of the work on themselves, those with personality are a magnet for those whose souls long for life. You have to own up to the person you've become. Who you are, whether you will or no, has an inductive effect on others. To my mind this is all to the good, for if enough individuals become more conscious then the collective will too, and life on this earth will go on.

The guiding principle is this: Be the one through whom you wish to influence others. Mere talk is hollow. There is no trick, however artful, by which this simple truth can be evaded in the long run. The fact of being convinced, and not the things we are convinced of—that is what has always, and at all times, worked a change in others.

In my first year of university, Philosophy 101, an assignment was to write an essay on the ethical consequences of aberrant—defined as unconventional—thought or behavior. Plato? Socrates? I don't remember the context. I do recall the question, "What if everyone thought or acted as you do?"—and my cavalier feeling at the time: little me among so many, what's to worry?

That was more than forty years ago. I was a bright and charming extravert, psychologically naive and impossibly normal. I knew as little about myself as I did about the genetics of bean-sprouts or the mating habits of elephants, and cared less. Now I know that we cannot escape a collective responsibility for the things we say, do and think—their effect on others and subsequent events.

Vocation, Groups and Inflation

What is it in the end, asks Jung, that induces one to rise out of unconscious identity with the mass as out of a swathing mist? He suggests that it is due to many and various irrational factors, but particularly to something commonly called vocation:

> True personality is always a vocation and puts its trust in it as in God, despite its being, as the ordinary man would say, only a personal feeling. But vocation acts like a law of God from which there is no escape. The fact that many a man who goes his own way ends in ruin means nothing to one who has a vocation. He *must* obey his own law, as if it were a daemon whispering to him of new and wonderful paths. Anyone with a vocation hears the voice of the inner man: he is *called*.[137]

To have a vocation originally meant "to be addressed by a voice." Examples of this are to be found in the avowals of Old Testament prophets, but historical personalities such as Goethe and Napoleon made no secret of their feeling of vocation.

When I was studying in Zurich I listened for that voice. Was analytic work truly my vocation? If the voice called, would I hear? What if it did not? Or, almost worse, what if it did? I was mindful of the way Samuel became one of the elect:

> And it came to pass at that time . . . ere the lamp of God went out in the temple of the Lord, where the ark of God was, and Samuel was laid down to sleep;
>
> That the Lord called Samuel: and he answered, Here am I.
>
> And he ran unto Eli, and said, Here am I; for thou calledst me. And he said, I called not; lie down again. And he went and lay down.
>
> And the Lord called yet again, Samuel. And Samuel arose and went to Eli, and said, Here am I; for thou didst call me. And he answered, I called not, my son; lie down again. . . .
>
> And the Lord called Samuel again the third time. And he arose and went to Eli, and said, Here am I; for thou didst call me. And Eli perceived that the Lord had called the child.
>
> Therefore Eli said unto Samuel, Go, lie down: and it shall be, if he call thee, that thou shalt say, Speak, Lord; for thy servant heareth. So Samuel went and lay down in his place.

---

[137] "The Development of Personality," *Development of Personality,* CW 17, pars. 299ff.

And the Lord came, and stood, and called as at other times, Samuel, Samuel. Then Samuel answered, Speak; for thy servant heareth.[138]

That's more or less what happened to me. One night, just like Samuel, I distinctly heard my name called, not once but thrice, and then again.

"Speak!" I cried, leaping out of bed, "I do heareth!" I was ripe for holy orders before I heard my housemate snickering behind the door. We had a good old pillow fight then. Puers at heart. But having already accepted that God—a.k.a. the Self—moves in mysterious ways, it was not a great leap of faith to imagine my feckless friend as His unwitting messenger.

Jung goes on:

Vocation, or the feeling of it, is not, however, the prerogative of great personalities; it is also appropriate to the small ones all the way down to the "midget" personalities, but as the size decreases the voice becomes more and more muffled and unconscious. It is as if the voice of the daemon within were moving further and further off, and spoke more rarely and more indistinctly. The smaller the personality, the dimmer and more unconscious it becomes, until finally it merges indistinguishably with the surrounding society, thus surrendering its own wholeness and dissolving into the wholeness of the group.[139]

The "wholeness of the group" is not an oxymoron; it simply designates the original unconsciousness we all participate in before we have differentiated ourselves from the collective. Differentiation is necessary because the call to become whole is not heard en masse; in a group the inner voice is drowned out by convention, and one's personal vocation is overwhelmed by collective necessity.

Nevertheless, doing psychological work with groups has become very popular. In the sixties and seventies, there were so-called encounter groups and not much else. Nowadays there is group therapy for just about everything and everyone, from victims of abuse to abusers, from addicts to their partners, from those seeking collective solace for lost foreskin to those who feel guilty about eating over sinks. Clearly many

---

[138] 1 Sam. 3: 2-10, Authorized Version.
[139] "The Development of Personality," *The Development of Personality,* CW 17, par. 302.

people find real value in sharing their traumatic or deviant experiences. That is abreaction; it is cathartic and it has a place. However, it is a far remove from what is involved in the process of individuation.

This is not to deny the widespread desire to change and the genuine search for a transformative experience. But a temporarily heightened awareness does not equal rebirth. You may think you have been forever changed when you are merely inflated with an overdose of previously unconscious material. Many is the analysand who has come to me high as a kite after a weekend workshop and had to be peeled off the ceiling.

Jung acknowledged that one can feel transformed during a group experience, but he cautioned against confusing this with the real thing. He pointed out that the presence of many people together exerts great suggestive force due to the phenomenon of *participation mystique,* unconscious identification; hence in a crowd one risks becoming the victim of one's own suggestibility. Jung writes:

> If any considerable group of persons are united and identified with one another by a particular frame of mind, the resultant transformation experience bears only a very remote resemblance to the experience of individual transformation. A group experience takes place on a lower level of consciousness than the experience of an individual. This is due to the fact that, when many people gather together to share one common emotion, the total psyche emerging from the group is below the level of the individual psyche. If it is a very large group, the collective psyche will be more like the psyche of an animal, which is the reason why the ethical attitude of large organizations is always doubtful. The psychology of a large crowd inevitably sinks to the level of mob psychology. . . . In the crowd one feels no responsibility, but also no fear.[140]

Positive group experiences are certainly possible. They can spur a person to noble deeds or instill a feeling of solidarity with others. The group can give one a degree of courage, a bearing and dignity that may easily get lost in isolation. But in the long run such gifts are unearned and so do not last. Away from the crowd and alone, you are a different person and unable to reproduce the previous state of mind.

---

[140] "Concerning Rebirth," *The Archetypes and the Collective Unconscious,* CW 9i, par. 225.

For some people, dealing with what happens to them in the course of an ordinary day is either too difficult or too mundane, perhaps both. Group work and esoteric practices—crystals, vision quests, channeling and the like—are much more exciting. They tempt with promises none of us is immune to: deliverance from the woes of this world and escape from oneself. This has been as true for me as for anyone else. At various times in my life I have sought enlightenment in the study of astrology, graphology, palmistry, phrenology (bumps on the skull), Rosicrucianism, yoga and existentialism—all very interesting, but when it came to the crunch they were no help at all.

Hearing the call is a numinous experience. Such events always have a deep emotional resonance. Hitherto unconscious contents have become conscious. What was previously unknown is now known. That automatically results in an enlargement of the personality. Cults, sudden conversions and other far-reaching changes of mind—like Paul on the road to Damascus—have their origin in such experiences. Whether for good or ill, only time will tell. Consciousness is temporarily disoriented, life as one has known it is disrupted, and when the ego is particularly weak the entire personality may disintegrate.

The extreme possibility is schizophrenia, a splitting of the mind— multiple personalities with no central control, a free-for-all among the complexes. But the more common danger is inflation, an unavoidable concomitant of realizing new things about oneself.

Inflation is a psychological phenomenon that involves an extension of the personality beyond individual limits. This regularly happens in analysis, as ego-awareness lights up the dark, but it is common in everyday life as well. One example is the way in which people identify with their business or title, as if they themselves were the whole complex of social factors which in fact characterize only their position. This is an unwarranted extension of oneself, whimsically bestowed by others.

Here are two passages by Jung on inflation:

"Knowledge puffeth up," Paul writes to the Corinthians, for the new knowledge had turned the heads of many, as indeed constantly happens. The inflation has nothing to do with the *kind* of knowledge, but simply and solely with the fact that any new knowledge can so seize hold of a weak head that he no longer sees and hears anything else. He is hypnotized by it, and instantly believes he has solved the riddle of the universe. But that is equivalent to almighty self-conceit.[141]

An inflated consciousness is always egocentric and conscious of nothing but its own existence. It is incapable of learning from the past, incapable of understanding contemporary events, and incapable of drawing right conclusions about the future. It is hypnotized by itself and therefore cannot be argued with. It inevitably dooms itself to calamities that must strike it dead. Paradoxically enough, inflation is a regression of consciousness into unconsciousness. This always happens when consciousness takes too many unconscious contents upon itself and loses the faculty of discrimination, the *sine qua non* of all consciousness.[142]

Every step toward greater consciousness creates a kind of Promethean guilt. Through self-knowledge, the gods are, as it were, robbed of their fire; that is, something that was the property of unconscious powers is torn out of its natural context and subordinated to the whims of the conscious mind. The one who has "stolen" the new knowledge becomes alienated from others. The pain of this loneliness is the vengeance of the gods, for never again can one return to the fold. Prometheus's punishment was to be chained to the lonely cliffs of the Caucasus, forsaken of God and man; an eagle fed on his liver, and as much as was devoured during the day, that much grew again during the night.

Fortunately, few of us have to go through all that. The ancient notion of the liver as the seat of the soul may linger on, but nowadays common sense and the reactions of others to an assumed godlikeness are usually enough to bring one down to earth.

However, there is still the feeling of having been chosen, set apart. Thus anyone who has found his or her individual path is bound to feel estranged from those who have not. This is simply a particular case of what I have generally observed, that those who have worked on themselves don't care to spend much time with those who haven't. One might think this to be elitist, but it is only natural. With a sense of vocation comes the realization that your time on this earth is precious. You become reluctant to squander it on those who don't know who they are or

---

[141] "The Relations Between the Ego and the Unconscious," *Two Essays,* CW 7, par. 243, note 1.

[142] *Psychology and Alchemy,* CW 12, par. 563.

why they are here, and are not inclined to ask.

Those who hear the call and respond become redeemer personalities—leaders, heroes, beacons of hope for others. Individuals with personality have *mana*.[143] But beware of those who seek vaingloriously to capitalize on this aura, including especially yourself. Those with *mana* may seem to be in possession of an absolute truth, but in fact the main thing they have that distinguishes them from others is a bedrock sense of themselves and the resolve to obey the law that commands from within.

The Religious Dimension

There is a religious aspect to Jungian psychology that has been called soul-making. Analyst Marion Woodman describes it like this:

> Psychological work is soul work. . . . By soul, I mean the eternal part of us that lives in this body for a few years, the timeless part of ourselves that wants to create timeless objects like art, painting and architecture. Whenever the ego surrenders to the archetypal images of the unconscious, time meets the timeless. Insofar as those moments are conscious, they are psychological—they belong to the soul. . . . For me, soul-making is allowing the eternal essence to enter and experience the outer world through all the orifices of the body . . . so that the soul grows during its time on Earth. It grows like an embryo in the womb. Soul-making is constantly confronting the paradox that an eternal being is dwelling in a temporal body. That's why it suffers, and learns by heart.[144]

This is not to say that Jungian psychology is a religion. Jung himself adamantly denied anything of the sort. Yet he did believe that the human longing for consciousness is essentially a religious activity. In an essay identifying five prominent groups of instinctive factors—creativity, reflection, activity, sexuality and hunger—he included the religious urge as a subset of reflection.[145]

Moreover, Jung also believed that a neurosis in midlife is never cured without the development of a *religious attitude*. Reason, sound judgment

---

[143] *Mana* is a Melanesian word referring to a bewitching or numinous quality in gods and sacred objects. In individual psychology, Jung used the term "mana personality" to describe the inflationary result of assimilating previously unconscious contents.

[144] *Conscious Femininity: Interviews with Marion Woodman*, pp. 134f.

[145] "Psychological Factors in Human Behaviour," CW 8, pars. 235ff.

and common sense take us only so far on the journey of healing and self-discovery. They offer answers to the practical questions, but when it comes to psychic suffering they are silent. Hence Jung writes:

> Among all my patients in the second half of life—that is to say, over thirty-five—there has not been one whose problem in the last resort was not that of finding a religious outlook on life. It is safe to say that every one of them fell ill because he had lost what the living religions of every age have given to their followers, and none of them has been really healed who did not regain his religious outlook.[146]

Jung, himself a Swiss Protestant pastor's son who decried his father's mindless faith,[147] stressed that he was by no means referring to belief in a particular creed or membership of a church, but rather to a certain attitude of mind. He described this attitude in terms of the Latin word *religio,* from *relegere,* meaning a careful consideration and observation of irrational factors historically conceived as spirits, demons, gods, etc., "the attitude peculiar to a consciousness which has been changed by experience of the *numinosum.* "—the unknown.[148]

Thus someone in a conflict situation, for instance, has to rely on

> divine comfort and mediation . . . . an autonomous psychic happening, a hush that follows the storm, a reconciling light in the darkness . . . secretly bringing order into the chaos of his soul.[149]

Jung often used the word "soul" in its traditional theological sense, but he strictly limited its psychological meaning. "By soul," he writes, "I understand a clearly demarcated functional complex that can best be described as 'personality.' "[150] Soul-making, in this secular sense, can thus be seen as a natural consequence of differentiating and consciously assimilating previously unconscious contents—particularly those associated with persona, shadow, and anima or animus.

Myself, I am temperamentally prosaic. I am so taken up with what is

---

[146] "Psychotherapists or the Clergy,"*Psychology and Religion,* CW 11, par. 509.

[147] See *Memories, Dreams, Reflections,* pp. 92ff. For a commentary on Jung's relationship with his father, see John P. Dourley, *A Strategy for a Loss of Faith,* pp. 13ff.

[148] "Psychology and Religion," *Psychology and Religion,* CW 11, par. 9.

[149] "A Psychological Approach to the Dogma of the Trinity," ibid., par. 260.

[150] "Definitions," *Psychological Types,* CW 6, par. 797.

right in front of me that I seldom think about soul from one day to the next. But when I do, yes, I can readily see my life in terms of soul— soulful encounters with my parts unknown. Clearly I have projected my soul onto many women, as have they onto me, and subsequently suffered its loss (as have they). Now I experience soul when I stare at the wall in the still of night. Soul is there when I am in conflict with myself, when I struggle for answers. Soul is what I am, as opposed to what I seem to be. Soul is forged in the interactions between me and my Rachel anima, and I see it daily in the material presented to me in my analytic practice.

Gordon, a forty-eight-year-old accountant, brings a dream:

> A woman approaches with a child. It's a boy, a year old, maybe a bit more. The woman is vaguely familiar. She asks me for religious instruction. I tell her she's made a mistake, that I'm an atheist. She just smiles and hands me the child.

"I woke up quite mystified. What do you make of it?" he asks.

"You first," I say.

"I suppose the woman is a feminine side of myself I don't know well."

"And the child?"

"New life, new possibilities . . . ? Say, it's just over a year ago that I started seeing you. That would have been the birth of something new, wouldn't it—the child?"

"And conception, nine months before that?"

"Well, let's see . . . that's when I left my wife . . ."

Maria, sixty-two-year-old artist, German by birth, survivor of an Allied concentration camp and an abusive childhood, taps the latest of the many thick journals in which for more than fifteen years she has kept a faithful record of her dreams, thoughts and daily happenings.

"This is my soul," she says. "It is me."

At times of transition from one stage of life to another, traditional religious imagery often appears in dreams. A childless woman in her forties dreams of baptizing her new-born. A man in his fifties dreams of finding a long-lost baby boy under a pile of rubble—in the basement of a church. People dream of being priests or nuns, of celebrating Mass, of family seders, of pilgrimages, of mountainous journeys, fearful descents into black holes, wandering in the desert. A shopping mall becomes a cathedral. Shrines magically appear in parking lots. Virgin births and divine children—born walking and speaking—are not rare.

The particular significance of such images is inextricably bound up with the dreamer's personal history and associations, but beyond that they seem to derive from a common bedrock, the archetypal basis for all mythology and all religion—the search for meaning. Hence Jung writes that a neurosis "must be understood, ultimately, as the suffering of a soul which has not discovered its meaning."[151]

Marie-Louise von Franz notes that Jung came early to the recognition that institutionalized religion could give him no answers. Instead, he found the way to illumination in the depths of himself; thus:

> The basis and substance of Jung's entire life and work do not lie in the traditions and religions which have become contents of collective consciousness, but rather in that primordial experience which is the source of these contents: the encounter of the single individual with his own god or daimon, his struggle with the emotions, affects, fantasies and creative inspirations and obstacles which come to light from within.[152]

The religious attitude can hardly be pinned down in a sentence or two, but it certainly involves acknowledging, and paying homage to, something numinous, mysterious—something far greater than oneself. God? Nature? The Self? Take your pick.

Analyst Lawrence Jaffe writes:

> Jung says of his message that it sounds like religion, but is not. He claims to be speaking as a philosopher, whereas on other occasions he rejected even that designation, preferring to be considered an empirical scientist. Consistently he rejected the idea that he was a religious leader—an understandable reaction in view of the usual fate of founders of new religions (like Christ): dismemberment and early death.
>
> Jung's protestations notwithstanding, his psychology can be considered a kind of religion; not a traditional religion with an emphasis on dogma, faith and ritual, to be sure, but a new kind—a religion of experience.[153]

Well, I can live with that, for when all is said and done, what is the

---

[151] "Psychotherapists or the Clergy," *Psychology and Religion,* CW 11, par. 497.
[152] *C.G. Jung,* pp. 13-14.
[153] *Liberating the Heart: Spirituality and Jungian Psychology,* p. 19.

wellspring of religion if not our experience of the gods? Nowadays we may call them complexes, but we might as well call them turnips. By any name they will always be essentially unknown. We may find these gods or complexes inside instead of out, but perhaps that is simply a manner of speaking. The alchemists saw little difference, according to this ancient Hermetic ditty quoted more than once by Jung:

Heaven above,
Heaven below.
Stars above,
Stars below.
All that is above
Also is below.
Grasp this
And rejoice.[154]

---

[154] See, for instance, "The Psychology of the Transference," *The Practice of Psychotherapy,* CW 16, par. 384.

Bibliography

Campbell, Joseph. *Hero with a Thousand Faces* (Bollingen Series XVII). Princeton: Princeton University Press, 1949.

Dalp, Sammlung. *Handschriften-deutung*. Bern: Franke Verlage, 1952.

Dourley, John P. *A Strategy for a Loss of Faith*. Toronto: Inner City Books, 1992.

Hillman, James. *Insearch: Psychology and Religion*. New York: Charles Scribner's Sons, 1967.

Jaffe, Lawrence W. *Liberating the Heart: Spirituality and Jungian Psychology*. Toronto: Inner City Books, 1990.

Jung, C.G. *C.G. Jung Letters* (Bollingen Series XCV). 2 vols. Ed. Gerhard Adler and Aniela Jaffé. Princeton: Princeton University Press, 1973.

_____. *The Collected Works* (Bollingen Series XX). 20 vols. Trans. R.F.C. Hull. Ed. H. Read, M. Fordham, G. Adler, Wm. McGuire. Princeton: Princeton University Press, 1953-1979.

_____. *Memories, Dreams, Reflections*. Ed. Aniela Jaffé. New York: Pantheon Books, 1961.

_____. *The Psychology of Kundalini Yoga: Notes of the Seminar Given in 1932* (Bollingen Series XCIX). Ed. Sonu Shamdasani. Princeton: Princeton University Press, 1996.

_____. *The Visions Seminars: Notes of the Seminars, 1930-1934*. Zürich: Spring Publications, 1976.

Kafka, Franz. *The Diaries of Franz Kafka, 1914-1923*. Trans. Martin Greenberg. Ed. Max Brod. London: Secker and Warburg, 1949.

_____. *Letters to Milena*. Trans. Tania and James Stern. New York: Schocken Books, 1966.

_____. *The Penal Colony: Stories and Short Pieces*. Trans. Willa and Edwin Muir. New York: Schocken Books, 1961.

Meier, C.A. *Ancient Incubation and Modern Psychotherapy*. Evanston, IL: Northwestern University Press, 1967.

Norman, Marsha. *The Fortune Teller*. New York: Bantam Books, 1988.

Plato. *The Symposium*. Trans. W.R.M. Lamb. Loeb Classical Library. Cambridge, MA: Harvard University Press, 1961.

Rilke, Rainer Maria. *The Notebook of Malte Laurids Brigge*. Trans. John Linton. London: The Hogarth Press, 1959.

_____. *Rilke on Love and Other Difficulties.* Ed. John Mood. New York: Norton, 1975.

Schoen, David. *Divine Tempest: The Hurricane As a Psychic Phenomenon.* Toronto: Inner City Books, 1998.

Sharp, Daryl. *Chicken Little: The Inside Story (A Jungian Romance).* Toronto: Inner City Books, 1993.

_____. *Dear Gladys: The Survival Papers, Book 2.* Toronto: Inner City Books, 1989.

_____. *Getting To Know You: The Inside Out of Relationship.* Toronto: Inner City Books, 1992.

_____. *Jung Lexicon: A Primer of Terms.* Toronto: Inner City Books, 1991.

_____. *Living Jung: The Good and the Better.* Toronto: Inner City Books, 1996.

_____. *Personality Types: Jung's Model of Typology.* Toronto: Inner City Books, 1987.

_____. *The Secret Raven: Conflict and Transformation in the Life of Franz Kafka.* Toronto: Inner City Books, 1980.

_____. *The Survival Papers: Anatomy of a Midlife Crisis.* Toronto: Inner City Books, 1988.

_____. *Who Am I, Really? Personality, Soul and Individuation.* Toronto: Inner City Books, 1995.

von Franz, Marie-Louise. *Alchemy: An Introduction to the Symbolism and the Psychology.* Toronto: Inner City Books, 1980.

_____. *C.G. Jung: His Myth in Our Time.* Trans. William H. Kennedy. Toronto: Inner City Books, 1998.

_____. *Puer Aeternus: A Psychological Study of the Adult Struggle with the Paradise of Childhood.* 2nd ed. Santa Monica, CA: Sigo Press, 1981.

_____. *Redemption Motifs in Fairytales.* Toronto: Inner City Books, 1980.

von Franz, Marie-Louise, and Hillman, James. *Lectures on Jung's Typology.* Zürich: Spring Publications, 1971.

Wilhelm, Richard, trans. *The I Ching or Book of Changes.* London: Routledge and Kegan Paul, 1968.

Woodman, Marion. *Conscious Femininity: Interviews with Marion Woodman.* Toronto: Inner City Books, 1993.

_____. *The Pregnant Virgin: A Process of Psychological Transformation.* Toronto: Inner City Books, 1985.

Index

Numbers in italics refer to illustrations

156